THE ISLAMIC DOCTRINE OF WOMEN

BILL WARNER, PHD

CENTER FOR THE STUDY OF
POLITICAL ISLAM

THE ISLAMIC DOCTRINE OF WOMEN

BILL WARNER, PHD

CENTER FOR THE STUDY OF
POLITICAL ISLAM

ISBN 0-9795794-9-X
ISBN13 978-0-9795794-9-3

V 09.14.2016

PUBLISHED BY CSPI, LLC
WWW.CSPIPUBLISHING.COM

PRINTED IN THE USA

TABLE OF CONTENTS

This book is dedicated to the
millions of victims of jihad over the past 1400 years.
May you read this and become a voice for the voiceless.

PREFACE

The Center for the Study of Political Islam (CSPI) teaching method is the easiest and quickest way to learn about Islam.

Authoritative

There are only two ultimate authorities about Islam—Allah and Mohammed. All of the curriculum in the CSPI method is from the Koran and the Sunna (the words and deeds of Mohammed). The knowledge you get in CSPI is powerful, authoritative and irrefutable. You learn the facts about the ideology of Islam from its ultimate sources.

Story-telling

Facts are hard to remember, stories are easy to remember. The most important story in Islam is the life of Mohammed. Once you know the story of Mohammed, all of Islam is easy to understand.

Systemic Knowledge

The easiest way to study Islam is to first see the whole picture. The perfect example of this is the Koran. The Koran alone cannot be understood, but when the life of Mohammed is added, the Koran is straight forward.

There is no way to understand Islam one idea at the time, because there is no context. Context, like story-telling, makes the facts and ideas simple to understand. The best analogy is that when the jig saw puzzle is assembled, the image on the puzzle is easy to see. But looking at the various pieces, it is difficult to see the picture.

Levels of Learning

The ideas of Islam are very foreign to our civilization. It takes repetition to grasp the new ideas. The CSPI method uses four levels of training to teach the doctrine in depth. The first level is designed for a beginner. Each level repeats the basics for in depth learning.

When you finish the first level you will have seen the entire scope of Islam, The in depth knowledge will come from the next levels.

Political Islam, Not Religious Islam

Islam has a political doctrine and a religious doctrine. Its political doctrine is of concern for everyone, while religious Islam is of concern only for Muslims.

Books Designed for Learning

Each CSPI book fits into a teaching system. Most of the paragraphs have an index number which means that you can confirm for yourself how factual the books are by verifying from the original source texts.

LEVEL 1

INTRODUCTION TO THE TRILOGY AND SHARIA

The Life of Mohammed, The Hadith, Lectures on the Foundations of Islam, The Two Hour Koran, Sharia Law for Non-Muslims, Self Study on Political Islam, Level 1

LEVEL 2

APPLIED DOCTRINE, SPECIAL TOPICS

The Doctrine of Women, The Doctrine of Christians and Jews, The Doctrine of Slavery, Self-Study on Political Islam, Level 2, Psychology of the Muslim, Factual Persuasion

LEVEL 3

INTERMEDIATE TRILOGY AND SHARIA

Mohammed and the Unbelievers, Political Traditions of Mohammed, Simple Koran, Self-Study of Political Islam, Level 3, Sources of the Koran, selected topics from *Reliance of the Traveller*

LEVEL 4

ORIGINAL SOURCE TEXTS

The Life of Muhammed, Guillaume; any *Koran, Sahih Bukhari,* selected topics, *Mohammed and Charlemagne Revisited,* Scott.

With the completion of Level 4 you are prepared to read both popular and academic texts.

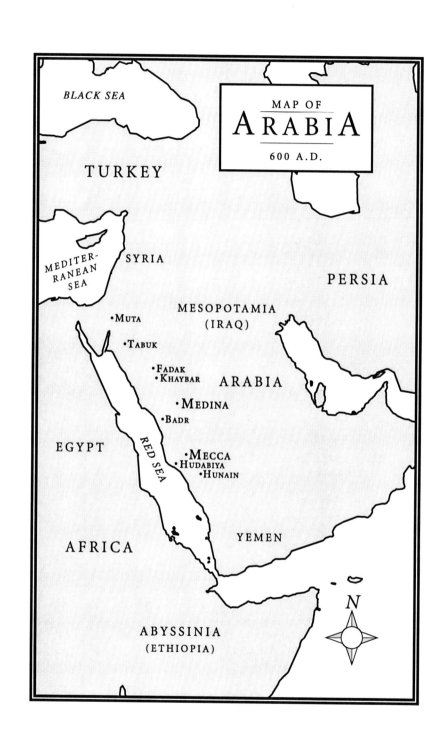

BLACK SEA

TURKEY

MAP OF
ARABIA
600 A.D.

MEDITER-
RANEAN
SEA

SYRIA

PERSIA

MESOPOTAMIA
(IRAQ)

•MUTA

•TABUK

•FADAK
•KHAYBAR

ARABIA

•MEDINA

•BADR

EGYPT

RED SEA

•MECCA
•HUDABIYA
•HUNAIN

AFRICA

YEMEN

N

ABYSSINIA
(ETHIOPIA)

OVERVIEW

CHAPTER 1

This book collects Islam's extensive doctrine of women as found in the sacred texts of Islam. Nearly every paragraph is taken from the most authoritative texts. What is found here is the very foundation of Islam and how women are treated in Islamic society.

THE ISLAMIC BIBLE—THE TRILOGY

Islam is defined by the words of Allah in the Koran, and the words and actions of Mohammed, called the *Sunna*.

The Sunna is found in two collections of texts—the Sira (Mohammed's life) and the Hadith (events in Mohammed's life). The Koran says 91 times that Mohammed's words and actions are considered to be the divine pattern for humanity.

A hadith, or tradition, is a brief story about what Mohammed did or said. A collection of hadiths is called a Hadith. There are many collections of hadiths, but the most authoritative are those by Bukhari and Abu Muslim, the ones used in this book.

So the Trilogy is the Koran, the Sira and the Hadith. Most people think that the Koran is the bible of Islam, but it is only about 14% of the total textual doctrine. The Trilogy is the foundation and totality of Islam.

FIGURE 1.1: THE RELATIVE SIZES OF THE TRILOGY TEXTS

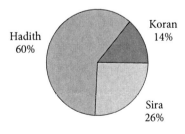

FIGURE 1.2: THE SUNNA OF MOHAMMED

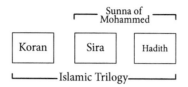

No one text of the Trilogy can stand by itself; it is impossible to understand any one of the texts without the other supporting texts. The Koran, Sira, and Hadith are a seamless whole and speak with one voice. If it is in the Trilogy, it is Islam.

KAFIR

The word Kafir will be used in this book instead of "unbeliever", the standard usage. Unbeliever is a neutral term. The Koran defines the Kafir and Kafir is not a neutral word. A Kafir is not merely someone who does not agree with Islam, but a Kafir is evil, disgusting, the lowest form of life. Kafirs can be deceived, hated, enslaved, tortured, killed, lied to and cheated. So the usual word "unbeliever" does not reflect the political reality of Islam.

There are many religious names for Kafirs: polytheists, idolaters, People of the Book (Christians and Jews), Buddhists, atheists, agnostics, and pagans. Kafir covers them all, because no matter what the religious name is, they can all be treated the same. What Mohammed said and did to polytheists can be done to any other category of Kafir.

Islam devotes a great amount of energy to the Kafir. The majority (64%) of the Koran is devoted to the Kafir, and nearly all of the Sira (81%) deals with Mohammed's struggle with them. The Hadith (Traditions) devotes 37% of the text to Kafirs[1]. Overall, the Trilogy devotes 51% of its content to the Kafir.

1—http://cspipublishing.com/statistical/TrilogyStats/AmtTxtDevotedKafir.html

FIGURE 1.3: AMOUNT OF TEXT DEVOTED TO KAFIR

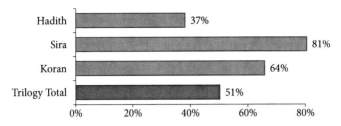

Here are a few examples in the Koran:

A Kafir can be mocked—

Koran 83:34 *On that day the faithful will mock the Kafirs, while they sit on bridal couches and watch them. Should not the Kafirs be paid back for what they did?*

A Kafir can be beheaded—

Koran 47:4 *When you encounter the Kafirs on the battlefield, cut off their heads until you have thoroughly defeated them and then take the prisoners and tie them up firmly.*

A Kafir can be plotted against—

Koran 86:15 *They plot and scheme against you [Mohammed], and I plot and scheme against them. Therefore, deal calmly with the Kafirs and leave them alone for a while.*

A Kafir can be terrorized—

Koran 8:12 *Then your Lord spoke to His angels and said, "I will be with you. Give strength to the believers. I will send terror into the Kafirs' hearts, cut off their heads and even the tips of their fingers!"*

A Muslim is not the friend of a Kafir—

Koran 3:28 *Believers should not take Kafirs as friends in preference to other believers. Those who do this will have none of Allah's protection and will only have themselves as guards. Allah warns you to fear Him for all will return to Him.*

A Kafir is cursed—

Koran 33:61 *They [Kafirs] will be cursed, and wherever they are found, they will be seized and murdered. It was Allah's same practice with those who came before them, and you will find no change in Allah's ways.*

KAFIRS AND PEOPLE OF THE BOOK

Muslims tell Christians and Jews that they are special. They are "People of the Book" and are brothers in the Abrahamic faith. But in Islam you are a Christian, if and only if, you believe that Christ was a man who was a prophet of Allah; there is no Trinity; Jesus was not crucified nor resurrected and that He will return to establish Sharia law. Nothing in Christian doctrine agrees with the Islamic definition of what a Christian is.

Under Islam, to be a true Jew you must believe that the Torah is corrupt and Mohammed is the last in the line of Jewish prophets.

This verse can be seen as positive:

> Koran 5:77 *Say: Oh, People of the Book, do not step out of the bounds of truth in your religion, and do not follow the desires of those who have gone wrong and led many astray. They have themselves gone astray from the even way.*

Islamic doctrine is dualistic, so there is an opposite view as well. Here is the last verse written about the People of the Book. [You cannot understand the Koran without knowing the principle of *abrogation*. The Koran has many contradictory verses. Abrogation says that the later verse is stronger or better than an earlier verse.] Since chapter 9 is the final chapter of the Koran, the last one written, it is the final word. It is stronger than all of the "peaceful" verses that precede it. It calls for Muslims to make war on the People of the Book who do not believe in the religion of truth, Islam.

> Koran 9:29 *Make war on those who have received the Scriptures [Jews and Christians] but do not believe in Allah or in the Last Day. They do not forbid what Allah and His Messenger have forbidden. The Christians and Jews do not follow the religion of truth until they submit and pay the poll tax [jizya] and they are humiliated.*

The sentence "They do not forbid..." means that they do not accept Sharia law; "until they submit" means submission to Sharia law.

In Islam, Christians and Jews are called infidels and "People of the Book"; Hindus are polytheists and pagans. The terms infidel, People of the Book, pagan and polytheist are religious words. Only the word "Kafir" shows the common political treatment of the Christian, Jew, Hindu, Buddhist, animist, atheist and humanist. What is done to a pagan can be done to a Christian, Jew or any other Kafir.

It is simple. If you don't believe that Mohammed is the prophet of Allah, then you are a Kafir.

The word Kafir will be used in this book instead of "unbeliever", "non-Muslim" or "disbeliever". Unbeliever or non-Muslim are neutral terms, but Kafir is not a neutral word. It is extremely bigoted and biased.

THE THREE VIEWS OF ISLAM

There are three points of view in dealing with Islam. The point of view you have depends upon how you feel about Mohammed. If you believe Mohammed is the prophet of Allah, then you are a believer. If you don't, you are a Kafir. The third viewpoint is that of a Kafir who is an apologist for Islam.

Apologists do not believe that Mohammed was a prophet, but they never say anything that would displease a Muslim. Apologists never offend Islam and condemn any analysis that is critical of Islam as being biased.

Let us give an example of the three points of view.

In Medina, Mohammed sat all day long beside his 12-year-old wife while they watched as the heads of 800 Jews were removed by sword.[2] Their heads were cut off because they had said that Mohammed was not the prophet of Allah. Muslims view these deaths as necessary because denying Mohammed's prophet-hood was an offense against Islam, and beheading is the accepted method of punishment, sanctioned by Allah.

Kafirs look at this event as proof of the jihadic violence of Islam and as an evil act. They call it ethnic cleansing.

Apologists say that this was a historic event, that all cultures have violence in their past, and that no judgment should be passed. They ignore the Islamic belief that the Sunna, Mohammed's words and deeds in the past, is the perfect model for today and tomorrow and forever. They ignore the fact that this past event of the beheading of 800 Jewish men continues to be acceptable in the present and the future.

According to the different points of view, killing the 800 Jews was either evil, a perfect godly act or only another historical event, take your pick.

This book is written from the Kafir point of view and is therefore, Kafir-centric. Everything in this book views Islam from how it affects Kafirs, non-Muslims. This also means that the religion is of little importance. Only a Muslim cares about the religion of Islam, but all Kafirs are affected by Islam's political views.

Notice that there is no right and wrong here, merely different points of view that cannot be reconciled. There is no possible resolution between

---

2   *The Life of Muhammad*, A. Guillaume, Oxford University Press, 1982, pg. 464.

the view of the Kafir and the Muslim. The apologist tries to bring about a bridge building compromise, but it is not logically possible.

MAXIM

Islam is primarily a political ideology. No action or statement by Islam can be understood without understanding its origins in the Trilogy. Any analysis, statement, or opinion about Islam is incomplete without a reference to the Trilogy. The Trilogy is the source and basis of all Islamic politics, diplomacy, history, philosophy, religion, and culture.

THE REFERENCE SYSTEM

This book is unusual in that it does two things at once. It is the simplest book you can read to learn about the real Mohammed. At the same time it is an authoritative biography because of the use of reference numbers. [Don't worry about these numbers. If you ignore them it doesn't make any difference. They are there in case you want to confirm what you have read or want to know more. The number allows you look it up in the source text. It is similar to a chapter/verse.] Here is an example:

I125 Mohammed made a decision that would have pleased Solomon. He...

The I in "I 125" tells you that it comes from Ishaq, the most authoritative writer of the Sira. The 125 is a reference number printed in the margin of the Sira. (*The Life of Muhammad*, A. Guillaume)

Other references within this work:

M123 is a page reference to W. Muir, *The Life of Mohammed*, AMS Press, 1975.

2:123 is a reference to the Koran, chapter 2, verse 123.

B1,3,4 is a reference to *Sahih Bukhari*, volume 1, book 3, number 4.

M012, 1234 is a reference to *Sahih Muslim*, book 12, number 1234.

THE WOMAN

5:92 Obey Allah, and obey the Messenger,
and be on your guard.

- A woman's highest achievement is motherhood.
- Men and women will be judged equally on Judgment Day.
- The veil and clothing are to be used to conceal a woman's sexuality.
- A woman's behavior during her menstrual cycle must be controlled by men.
- Most of the people in Hell will be women.
- Women are less intelligent than men.
- Women have half the legal standing of a man.
- It is an insult to say that Allah has daughters.
- Islam forbids killing female children.

There is a major political division between Islam and the rest of the world. The political duality is:

dar al Islam (land of submission) and
dar al harb (land of war).

Islam's duality at the personal level is between the Muslim and the Kafir.

The major duality inside Islam is male/female. There is one set of rules for men and another set of rules from women. If there were no submission, then there would need to be only one rule: men and women are treated the same. If they are not to be treated the same, then many more rules are needed.

There is only one area in which men and women are treated equally—both sexes will be judged on the basis of their lives on Judgment Day.

There is not very much material in the Trilogy about females. Only about 9% of the Koran and about 12% of the Sira refers to females. The overwhelming amount of the doctrine is about men. But there is more than enough in the Trilogy to govern the smallest detail in the life of a woman from birth to death.

WOMAN AS MOTHER

There is only one way in which a woman is held to be superior to a man: if, and only if, a woman is a mother, is she held in higher esteem than a man.

> Koran 46:15 *We command man to show kindness to his parents. His mother bore and gave birth to him in pain. From birth to weaning is thirty months; when he reaches full strength at forty years of age, he says, "My Lord, open my heart so that I may be grateful for the favor You have given me and my parents and so that I will do the good works that please You. Be gracious to me in my offspring; I have turned to you and do surrender to Islam."*

EQUALITY

On Judgment Day both male and female will be judged on the basis of what they have done in their lives. However, as it will become clear from the following material, since a woman must submit to the man in all things, she will be judged by how well she submitted during her life.

> Koran 16:97 *Whoever does good, whether male or female, and believes, We will certainly give a happy life, and We will certainly give them their reward for the best of their actions.*

This next verse is the high point of Islamic relations between the sexes. Women will be "rewarded by their actions," which must include submission to men.

> Koran 9:71 *The faithful of both sexes are mutual friends. They command what is just and forbid what is evil. They observe regular prayer, contribute regularly to charity, and they obey Allah and His Messenger. Allah will show His mercy to these. Allah is mighty and wise. Allah promised the faithful, both men and women, Gardens beneath which the rivers flow in which they shall abide, and blessed mansions in the Gardens.*

THE VEIL

The veil has many manifestations, burka, purdah, hijab, but they are all methods of hiding and secluding the woman from society.

Here we see that young girls and menstruating women were secluded in Mohammed's community.

> [B2,15,88;B2,15,91]
> *Um Atiya said that on the Day of Id [a festival], women were told to come out behind the men and say Takbir and invoke Allah with them. Also included were the menstruating women and young virgins who would normally be in seclusion.*

Mohammed's wives were all veiled. In the following hadith.

> [B1,4,148;B8,74,257]
> *The wives of the Prophet used to go to a large open place to answer the call of nature at night. Umar used to say to the Prophet "Let your wives be veiled," but Allah's Apostle did not do so. One night Sauda went out at night and she was a tall lady. Umar said, "I have recognized you, O Sauda."*
>
> *He said he desired that the women might be veiled. So Allah revealed the verses of veiling.*

A woman should be hidden from all men who might have sex with them. Only their relatives and slaves can know their private lives.

> Koran 33:55 *There is no blame on the Messenger's wives if they speak unveiled with their fathers, sons, brothers, nephews on either their brother's or sister's side, their women, or their slave-girls. Women! Fear Allah, for Allah witnesses all things.*

Here we see that the seclusion of the veil is all about sex.

> Koran 24:60 *As for the unmarried women past the age of childbearing, they will not be blamed it they take off their outer garments, as long as they do not show their adornments [jewelry]. It will be better for them if they do not take them off, for Allah hears and knows all.*

MENSTRUATION

A menstruating woman is unclean and is restricted as to what she can do.

> [B1,4,227;B1,6,304;B1,6,305]
> *A woman came to Mohammed and asked, "If anyone of us gets menses in her clothes then what should she do?" He replied, "She should take hold of the soiled place, put it in water and rub it in order to remove the traces of blood and then pour more water over it. Then she can pray in it."*

Menstruation makes a woman unclean.

> Koran 2:222 *They ask you about women's menstrual cycle. Say: It is a discomfort. Therefore, keep away from them during this time and do not come near them until they are clean again. But when they are clean, you may lie with them as Allah has commanded. Allah loves those who turn to Him and seek cleanliness.*

THE STATUS OF WOMEN

It is the nature of females that most of those in Hell will be women.

[B1,4,184;B1,12,712;B2,18,154;B2,18,156;B2,18,157;B2,18,159;B2,18,161;B2,18,162;B2, 18,164;B3;40,552;B4,54,423;B7,62,125;B9,92,390]

[...]

Mohammed's followers then told him that during his prayer they saw him reach out with his hands and grasp something, and later retreat in horror. Mohammed replied, "I saw Paradise and stretched my hands towards a bunch of fruit, and had I taken it, you would have eaten from it as long as this world remains. I also saw Hellfire, and I have never seen such a terrible sight. I saw that the majority of the inhabitants were women." When asked why this was so, Mohammed replied, "They are ungrateful to their husbands and to good deeds. Even if you are good to one of them all of your life, whenever she sees some harshness from you she will say, 'I have never seen any good from you.'"

Mohammed also saw a woman in Hell being clawed by a cat. He learned that she had imprisoned a cat, neither feeding it nor allowing it to seek its own food, until it starved.

Women are less intelligent than men. They are also spiritually inferior to men.

[B1,2,28;B1,6,301;B2,24,541;B4,54,464;B7,62,124;B7,62,126;B7,76,456;B8,76,554 ;B8,76,555]

Once, after offering prayer at Musalla, Mohammed said to the women, "O women! Give alms, as I have seen that the majority of the dwellers of Hell were women." They asked, "Why is it so, O Allah's Apostle?" He replied, "You curse frequently and are ungrateful to your husbands. I have not seen anyone more deficient in intelligence and religion than you. A cautious sensible man could be led astray by some of you."

The women asked, "O Allah's Apostle! What is deficient in our intelligence and religion?" He replied, "Is not the evidence of two women equal to the witness of one man?" They agreed that this was so. He said, "This is the deficiency in her intelligence. Isn't it true that a woman can neither pray nor fast during her menses?" The women replied that this was so. He said, "This is the deficiency in her religion."

The religion of a women is controlled by the man.

[B6,61,572;B7,62,120]

Mohammed once said "A woman should not engage in optional fasts without her husband's permission if he is at home."

Women are an affliction to men.

[B4,52,111;B7,62,30;B7,62,31;B7,62,33;B7,62,32;B7,71,649;B7,71,666]
Mohammed said, "If at all there is a bad omen, it is in the horse, the woman and the house."

On another occasion, he had said, "I have not left any affliction after me more harmful to men than women."

Women cannot help their flaws, so be nice to them.

[B4,55,548;B7,62,113;B7,62,113]
Mohammed said, "Treat women nicely, for a women is created from a rib, and is much like one. If you try to straighten a rib, it will break, so I urge you to take care of the women."

A woman, a donkey or a dog can nullify prayers.

[B1,9,486;B1,9,490]
When told that a prayer is annulled if the praying ones are passed by a dog, a donkey, or a woman, Aisha said,

Do you make us women equal to dogs and donkeys? While I used to lie in my bed, the Prophet would sometimes come to pray facing the middle of the bed. I felt like it was wrong of me to remain in front of him while he prayed, so I would slip away slowly and quietly from the foot of the bed until I stopped feeling guilty.

Female leadership will lead to political failure.

[B9,88,219]
During the battle of Al-Jamal, Mohammed heard the news that the people of Persia had made the daughter of Khosrau their ruler. On this, he said, "A nation that makes a woman their ruler will never succeed."

LEGAL

The longest verse in the Koran is about contract law (Mohammed was a businessman). The general principle in Islamic law is that it takes two women to equal one man.

Koran 2:282 Believers! When you contract a loan for a certain period, write it down, or to be fair, let a scribe write it down. The scribe should not refuse to write as Allah has taught him; therefore, let the scribe record what the debtor dictates being mindful of his duty to Allah and not reducing the amount he owes. If the debtor is ignorant and unable to dictate, let his guardian do so with fairness. Call two men in to witness this, but if two men cannot be found, then call one man and two women whom you see fit to be witnesses. Therefore, if either woman makes an error, the other can correct her. Witnesses must not refuse to give testimony if they are called upon to do so; therefore, do not forget to record your debts in writing, whether they are little or much, along with the date on which they were paid. This is more fair in Allah's sight, as it ensures accuracy in proof and is the best way to avoid doubt. If, however, the transaction is one that occurs on the spot, you are not to blame if it is not recorded in writing. And have witnesses when you sell, and do not let harm come to the scribe or witnesses for it will be a sin for you if this occurs. And fear Allah and Allah will give you knowledge for He has knowledge of all things.

In this verse about estates, we have another application of the principle that a woman is half of a man.

Koran 4:11 It is in this manner that Allah commands you concerning your children: A male should receive a share equal to that of two females, and if there are more than two females, they should receive two-thirds of what the deceased has left. If there is only one female, she will inherit half. The father and mother of the deceased will each receive a sixth of what is left if he has a child, but if he has no children, his parents are his heirs, and his mother should receive a third. If he has brothers, his mother will only receive a sixth, after paying his inheritances and debts. You may not know whether your parents or your children are more useful, but this is Allah's law. Allah is knowing and wise!

THE DAUGHTERS OF ALLAH

In the Koran of Mecca, there are five references to Allah's denial of having daughters. The background is that there were three goddesses who were part of the worship at the Kabah of Mecca. The Meccans also said that angels were females.

Koran 53:19 Do you see Al-Lat and Al-Ozza, and Manat [Arabic deities] the third idol? What? Do you have male children and Allah female children [Arabs called angels the daughters of Allah]? That is an unfair division! Koran53:23 These are mere names. You and your fathers gave them these names. Allah has not acknowledged them. They follow only their own conceits and desires, even though their Lord has already given them guidance.

It is evil to suggest that Allah has any partners, but it is even worse to imply that Allah has daughters.

Koran16:57 Glory be to Him! They wish for sons, and they say that Allah has daughters [the Meccans considered the angels to be the daughters of Allah]. If they receive news that they have a daughter, their face darkens and they are filled with anguish. They hide themselves from their people in shame. Should they keep the child in shame or simply bury it? What an evil choice they make for themselves.

Koran 17:40 *What? Has your Lord honored you by giving you sons while He has taken for Himself daughters from among the angels? Truly, you say a dreadful thing.*

BURYING DAUGHTERS

Islam claims to have greatly improved women's rights. Whatever improvement Islam made was a limited improvement since the Trilogy is eternal, universal and perfect. In short, whatever improvement Islam made in the condition of women 1400 years ago, is done. No more improvement to be done. "Eternal" and "perfect" do not allow for improvement.

We can see what female life was like before Islam by looking at Mohammed's wife Khadija. Before she met Mohammed, she was independently wealthy, ran her own business, owned slaves and other property, proposed her own marriage, inherited property, loaned money and was not secluded behind a curtain.

One of the ways that Islam claims to have improved the status of women is to prevent the "burying of daughters". The Koran states that very poor Arabs would bury female babies alive. Both the Koran and the Hadith condemn this practice.

[B3,41,591;B8,73,6;B8,76,480;B9,92,395]
According to Al-Mughira, Mohammed used to forbid idle talk, asking too many questions about religion, wasting money, not giving what should be given in charity, and asking others for something (except in great need), extravagance, being undutiful to mothers, and burying one's little daughters alive.

This is the Sunna of Mohammed

MARRIAGE

CHAPTER 3

*4:59 Believers! Obey Allah and obey His Messenger
and those among you with authority.*

- A Muslim woman has many regulations as to whom she can marry.
- The woman receives a dowry.
- The main element a woman brings to marriage is sex.
- A woman must have sex whenever a man wants it.
- Divorce is determined by the man.
- A man may have up to four wives.

The marriage in Islam is not like that of Western civilization. Marriage is a civil contract exactly like any business contract. There does not even have to be a religious ceremony.

One of the great strengths of Islam is how it makes marriage and having children a center of Islamic civilization. Not only is marriage encouraged, but celibacy is condemned. Marriage is called half of a Muslim's religion. To be healthy and unmarried is to be a brother of Satan. When a Muslim reaches puberty he should marry.

> [B7,62,173]
> Mohammed said to Jabir, "If you enter your town at night after coming from a journey, do not enter upon your family till your wife shaves her pubic hair and combs her hair. O Jabir! Seek to have offspring, seek to have offspring!"

QUALIFICATIONS

A Muslim woman cannot be married against her will.

> [B7,62,67;B7,62,68;B9,85,79;B9,86,98]
> Aisha asked Mohammed, "O Allah's Apostle! Should women be asked for their consent to their marriage?" When he replied that they should, Aisha said, "A virgin, if asked, feels shy and keeps quiet." He said, "Her silence expresses her consent."

A Muslim woman may not marry a Kafir. Pagan (not a Jew or Christian) women may not be married to a Muslim male.

> Koran 2:221 *You will not marry pagan women unless they accept the faith. A slave girl who believes is better than an idolatress, although the idolatress may please you more. Do not give your daughters away in marriage to Kafirs until they believe, for a slave who is a believer is better than an idolater, though the idolater may please you more.*

THE CONTRACT

The marriage dowry is not refundable.

> Koran 4:20 *If you want to exchange one wife for another, do not take anything away from the dowry you have given her. Would you take it by slandering her and doing her obvious wrong? How could you take it back when you have slept with one another and entered into a firm covenant?*

Marriage always includes the business of the dowry (mahr) paid to the bride.

A man may have from one to four wives and as many slave-girls as he wishes.

> Koran 4:3 *If you fear that you will not be able to deal with orphan girls fairly, marry other women of your choice, two, or three, or four; but if you fear that you cannot treat them equally, then marry only one, or any of the slave-girls you have acquired. This will prevent you from being unjust.*

MARITAL SEX

The most important thing that a woman brings to the marriage is her vagina.

> [B3,31,129;B7,62,81]
> *Mohammed said:*
> *He who can afford to marry should marry, because it will help him refrain from looking at other women, and save his private parts from looking at other women, and save his private parts from committing illegal sexual relations; and he who cannot afford to marry is advised to fast, as fasting will diminish his sexual power.*
> *He also said, "The stipulations of the marriage contract most entitled to be abided by are those with which you are given the right to enjoy a woman's private parts."*

Allah curses the woman who resists sex.

[B4,54,460;B7,62,121;B7,62,122;]
Mohammed said, "If a husband calls his wife to his bed for sex and she refuses and causes him to sleep in anger, the angels will curse her till morning."

This next hadith and verse clearly give the status of a Muslim woman. A Muslim wife is always ready to have sex upon demand. It is her husband's right. Plowed fields is an Islamic term for the vagina, an interesting agricultural image.

M008,3363
Jabir said that the Jews had an expression which said, "When a man has sex with his wife from behind, their child will have squinty eyes." Consequently, the verse was revealed,

Koran 2:223 Your women are your tilth (plowed fields, vagina): go into your fields when you like, but do some good deed beforehand and fear Allah. Keep in mind that you will meet Him. Give good news to the believers.

M008,3365
Mohammed: "It is all right if a man wants to enter his wife from behind or from on top, but he should enter the vagina."

THE HOME

When a woman is out of the house, she should be accompanied by a relative. And the woman cannot have a man in her house who is not related to her if her husband is not at home. The sexuality of a woman is to be controlled at all times. Absolute control of a woman's sexuality in all of its forms is part of a man's ghira (pride, honor, self-respect and sacred jealousy).

[B2,20,192;B2,20,193;B3,29,85;B3,31,215]
Mohammed said that a woman is forbidden from traveling for two or more days without her husband or a Dhi-Mahram (a man she cannot marry by Islamic law).

It is the husband or father who determines who comes into the house. It is not allowed for a wife or daughter to exercise this choice. Exercising this power is part of a man's ghira (see next section, Jealousy and Honor).

[B1,2,53;B2,24,506;B2,24,518;B2,24,520;B2,24,521;B2,24,546;B3,34,279;B3,34,280;B7,6
2,123;B7,64,273]

*Mohammed said, "You will be rewarded for whatever you
spend for Allah's sake even if it were a morsel which you put in your
wife's mouth." As Mohammed told the wife of Abu Salama, this
also counts for what one spends to feed one's own children: "Spend
on them and you will get a reward for what you spend on them."*

*"If a lady gives meals (in charity) from her husband's house
without spoiling her husband's property," Mohammed added, "she
will get a reward and her husband will also get a reward likewise,
as will the storekeeper. The husband will get a reward because of
his earnings and the woman because of her spending. The reward
of one will not decrease the reward of the others."*

*Also, Mohammed said that if a wife gives some of her husband's
property without his permission, he will receive half of the reward.*

*She may not fast without his permission if he is at home, and she
must not allow anyone to enter his house without his permission.*

The wife should always be allowed to go the mosque.

[B1,12,824;B2,13,22;

*Mohammed said, "If your women ask permission to go to the
mosque at night, allow them."*

If a man brings a new wife into the home, here is the law for the new wife.

[B7,62,140;B7,62,141]

*It is Mohammed's tradition that if someone marries a virgin
and he already has a matron wife then he should stay for seven
days with the virgin and then alternate between the two; converse-
ly, if someone marries a matron and he already has a virgin wife
then he should stay with the matron for three days and then alternate the two.*

JEALOUSY AND HONOR—GHIRA

In this hadith we have the basis for a Muslim's sense of honor and pride.
The man rules the woman, and his status in the community depends upon
how his women conduct themselves. Ghira is sacred jealousy, even Allah has ghira. Ghira is also self-respect and is the basis of honor killings.
Notice that Saed's threat to kill a man with his wife is not condemned, but
supported. Violence in defence of a Muslim's ghira is pure Islam.

[B8,82,829;B9,93,512]

*Saed bin Ubada said, "If I saw a man with my wife, I would
strike him with the blade of my sword." This news reached*

Mohammed, who then said, "You people are astonished at Saed's ghira (self-respect). By Allah, I have more ghira than he, and Allah has more ghira than I, and because of Allah's ghira, He has made unlawful shameful deeds and sins done in open and in secret.

And there is none who likes more that the people should repent to Him and beg His pardon than Allah, and for this reason He sent the admonishers and the givers of good news. And there is none who likes to be praised more than Allah does, and for this reason, Allah promised to grant Paradise to the doers of good."

THE RIGHTS OF A WOMAN

Islam is very clear on a woman's rights. Mohammed talked about this in his last sermon at Mecca. If a woman obeys her husband and never acts in a sexual manner towards another man (including being alone with another male), then she must be given food and shelter. [All quotes with the number starting with I are from Ishaq, the Sira.]

1969 Mohammed also told them men had rights over their wives and women had rights over their husbands. The wives were never to commit adultery or act in a sexual manner toward others. If they did, they were to be put in separate rooms and beaten lightly. [Stoning is the penalty in other hadiths.] If they refrained from what was forbidden, they had the right to food and clothing. Men were to lay injunctions on women lightly for they were prisoners of men and had no control over their persons.

Again, from the Sira, we have some more about a husband's rights:

1957 Mohammed sent Muadh to Yemen to proselytize. While he was there he was asked what rights a husband has over the wife. He replied to the woman who asked, "If you went home and found your husband's nose running with pus and blood and you sucked it until it was cleaned, you still would not have fulfilled your husband's rights."

DIVORCE, DEATH AND REMARRIAGE

Before there is a divorce, the families should try to resolve the problem.

Koran 4:35 If you fear a breach between a man and wife, then send a judge from his family, and a judge from her family. If they both want to come to a reconciliation, Allah will bring them back together. Truly Allah is all-knowing and wise!

There is a period of time called *iddah* that a woman must wait after the divorce before she can remarry.

[B7,63,256]

Ibn Abbas interpreted the Koranic verse 2.240 as a cancellation of the order that a woman must spend the period of iddah (mourning for one's husband) in her husband's house. He must provide for her to stay at his house for one year in his will, but if she leaves, his family is no longer obligated to care for her.

[B5,59,326;B6,60,52;B6,60,54;B6,60,55;B7,62,61;B7,63,239;B7,63,240;B7,63,241;B7,63,248]

Allah proclaimed that a woman separated from her husband by his death must wait for a period of four months and ten days (or three menstrual cycles) before she could marry again. This period, also required after a woman is divorced, is called the iddah, and was revealed in the verse:

Koran 2:232 When you have divorced a woman and she has fulfilled the period of waiting, iddah, do not interfere with her marrying a new husband if it has been agreed between them honorably. This is commanded for everyone who has faith in Allah and the Last Day; this course of action is more virtuous and pure. Allah knows and you do not.

Subaia, whose husband Sad died while she was pregnant, gave birth soon afterward and prepared herself for suitors. Abu As-Sanabil said to her, "I see you dressed up for the people to ask you in marriage. Do you want to marry? By Allah, you are not allowed to marry unless four months and ten days have elapsed." That evening, Subaia went to Mohammed and asked him about this problem. He said that she was free to marry because she had already given birth to her child.

The sister of Maqil was married to a man who divorced her and remained away until she had completed her iddah. He then sought to marry her again, and this angered Maqil, who refused to allow the marriage. Then Allah revealed the Iddhah verse. Mohammed recited this verse to Maqil, and so he yielded to Allah's command.

The mahr is the dowry. It does not have to be returned, but here the wife returns the garden (mahr), and she gets to have her divorce.

[B7,63,197;B7,63,198;B7,63,199]

The wife of Thabit came to Mohammed and said, "O Allah's Apostle! I do not blame Thabit for defects in his character or his religion, but I am afraid I would behave in un-Islamic manner and become unthankful for Allah's blessings." On that Mohammed said, "Will you give back the garden which your husband has given you as mahr?" She said, "Yes." Then the Prophet said to Thabit, "O Thabit! Accept your garden, and divorce her at once."

This hadith gives an option of a semi-divorce. The "wife" has no sexual rights, but has a roof and food. Mohammed had two wives who "gave up their turn" in order to remain in the household, but had no sex with him. In their case, they also got an assured seat in Paradise along with all of Mohammed's wives.

[B3,43,630;B3,49,859;B6,60,125;B7,62,134]
Aisha explained the meaning of the Koran verse:

Koran 4:128 And if a wife fears cruelty or desertion from her husband, then they are not to blame for coming to a mutual agreement between themselves, for peace is best, although people are often prone to greed. But if you do good and fear Allah; Allah knows all that you do. As hard as you try to treat all your wives equally, you cannot. Do not abandon one of them altogether, so as to leave her hanging in suspense. If you come to a mutual agreement and fear Allah, then truly Allah is forgiving and merciful. But if they separate, Allah will provide for the both of them from His abundance; Allah is vast and wise.

She said that it concerns the woman whose husband does not want to keep her with him any longer, but wants to divorce her and marry some other lady, so she says to him: "Keep me and do not divorce me, and then marry another woman, and you may neither spend on me, nor sleep with me."

There is an extensive amount of the Koran devoted to divorce.

Koran 33:49 Believers! If you marry a believing woman and divorce her before consummating the marriage, you do not have to wait out the prescribed term. Provide for her and dismiss her with honor.

This next verse allows for marriage to girls who have not reached puberty. The pregnant woman must wait until her child is born to get a divorce. ●

Koran 65:4 If you have doubt about your wives who have ceased to menstruate, the prescribed waiting period is three months. This length of time is also prescribed for young girls [wives] who have not yet menstruated. As for women who are pregnant, they must wait until they have given birth. Allah will make His command easy for those who fear Him. This is Allah's command which He has sent down to you. Whoever fears Allah will be forgiven of his sins and He will increase his reward.

Koran 65:6 *Keep your divorced wives in your home according to your means, and do not injure them so as to make life unbearable for them. If they are pregnant, keep them until they give birth. After that, if they breast-feed their children, pay them and seek mutual guidance together. But if you cannot agree, hire a wet-nurse for the child.*

Koran 2:226 *Those who abandon their wives on oath must wait four months. If they decide to return, Allah is forgiving and merciful. If, however, they decide to divorce them, remember that Allah hears and knows all.*

Men are a degree above women in legal rights.

Koran 2:228 *Divorced women must keep themselves from men for three menstrual periods. It is not lawful for them to hide what Allah has created in their wombs if they believe in Allah and the Last Day. If they are in that state, it is better for their husbands to take them back if they want reconciliation. Women have rights similar to those of men in regard to justice, but men are a degree above them. Allah is mighty and wise.*

The history behind the following verse is not known. After the third divorce the woman must marry a second man and have sex with him. Then she and the second man get a divorce and then she can remarry the first husband.

Koran 2:230 *If a husband divorces his wife for a third time, it is not lawful for him to take her back until she has married and divorced another husband. Then if they return to each other, it will not be a sin for either if they can keep within the limits set by Allah. Such are the limits set by Allah. He makes them clear for those who understand. But if you have divorced a woman and she has fulfilled the period of waiting, then either keep her honorably or let her leave with kindness. You must not keep her to do her evil or take advantage for if anyone does that, he harms his soul. Do not mock Allah's revelations, but remember the grace He has shown you and the Scriptures and the wisdom He has sent down as a warning. Fear Allah and know that Allah is all-knowing.*

It is the man who determines how long the baby will nurse the mother.

Koran 2:233 *Divorced mothers should breast-feed their children for two full years if the father wishes for the child to nurse that long. They should be cared for and clothed by the father during this time. No one should pay more than they can afford. A mother should not have to suffer for her child's sake nor should the father, and these duties are the same for the father's heir. But if it is agreed upon that the child should be weaned, they should not be blamed. If you decide to have a wet-nurse for your children, there is no blame if you pay her fairly. Fear Allah and know that Allah sees everything you do.*

MORE ABOUT MARRIAGE

Temporary marriage still exists today with the Shia Muslims.

[B7,62,52;B9,86,90]

Mohammed told the men in this army that they were allowed to engage in a muta marriage, which allows a man and a woman to agree to marry temporarily. During such, the marriage would last for three nights, and if they want it to continue, it can, or they can separate.

Not long thereafter, Mohammed decreed that the muta marriage was unlawful. Mohammed also forbade shingar marriage, which is when a man marries the daughter of a man in exchange for marrying his daughter to the man, without exchange of property (a dowry). It is also called shingar when such a marriage occurs with an exchange of sisters.

There is an implication in this hadith that husbands do not betray their wives.

[B4,55,547;B4,55,611]

Mohammed said, "If it were not for Eve, wives would never betray their husbands."

When the Meccans came to Medina, they were poor and the Medinans had to care for them. Mohammed made each Meccan a brother to a fellow Medinan. Here we see how generous one of the Medinans was. Sad gives away one of his wives like a piece of property.

[B3,34,264;B5,58,124;B5,58,125;B7,62,47;B8,75,395]

When Mohammed made a bond of fraternity between Abdur-Rahman and Sad, who was a rich man, Sad said, "The Ansar know that I am the richest of all of them, so I will divide my property into two parts between me and you. I have two wives; see which of the two you like so that I may divorce her and you can marry her after she becomes lawful to you by her passing the prescribed period of divorce. Abdur-Rahman said, "May Allah bless your family for you."

While he was trading in the market, Abdur-Rahman encountered Mohammed bearing the traces of yellow scent over his clothes. Mohammed asked him, "What is this scent?" He replied, "I have married a woman." Mohammed asked, "How much mahr (marriage gift) have you given?" Abdur-Rahman replied that he had given either gold amounting to the size of a date-stone or an actual golden date-stone; the sources are unsure. Mohammed told him, "Arrange a marriage banquet, even if just with a sheep."

Since Mohammed married a virgin and matrons, he had practical advice to give on the matter of which type was good for what service. We have another reference of her shaving the pubic hair.

> [B3,41,589;B4,52,211;B7,62,16;B7,62,17;B7,62,174;B7,64,280;B8,75,396]
> *Jabir was riding back toward Medina with Mohammed following a jihad battle and Mohammed asked why he was in such a hurry. Jabir said that he was newly married. Mohammed asked, "A virgin or a matron?" Jabir replied, "A matron." Mohammed said, "Why didn't you marry a young girl so that you could play with her and she with you?" Jabir said, "My father died and I have some young sisters, so I have married a matron so that she may serve them and teach them manners." On that Mohammed said, "May Allah bless you. That is good."*
>
> *When they neared Medina and were going to enter it, Mohammed said, "Wait till you enter your home early in the night so that the lady whose hair is unkempt may comb her hair and that the lady whose husband has been away may shave her pubic hair."*

A MARRIAGE STORY

There are many of these stories of how a Muslim used jihad for the purpose of getting the money for the mahr, the marriage dowry.

1990 A Muslim, Ibn Hadrad, was to marry and had proposed a dowry of 200 dirhams. He went to Mohammed and asked if he had such an amount. Mohammed said no. A man named Rifa was the head of the Jusham clan and was an enemy of Allah. So Mohammed sent Ibn Hadrad and two other men to get information about the tribe.

1990 The Muslims sneaked upon the Jusham camp and waited. To their good fortune Rifa left the camp to look for a lost shepherd. Ibn Hadrad shot him through the heart and the three Muslims then shouted, "Allah akbar," and charged into the camp with swords and the tribe fled. Ibn Hadrad cut off Jusham's head, took the livestock, and went back to Mohammed.

1991 Ibn Hadrad was given some of the livestock to sell and pay his dowry so he could consummate the marriage.

THE SHARIA LAW

The Sharia system of Islamic law is the practical conclusion of political Islam. It is also a way for the Kafir to see how the Trilogy forms the basis of not only for a religion but also for the most powerful political system in history. The Trilogy is both a political theory and a complete, detailed code of law that covers contract law, banking, family law, insurance, criminal law, and foreign policy.

The following is a summary from a thirteen-hundred-year-old classic text, *The Reliance of the Traveller*.[1] Due to the fact that the Koran is considered to be unchangingly perfect and final, this legal code is unchanging and is still used today. Once you have read the Koran and the Hadith, you will recognize all of these laws. They are nothing more than a codified summary of both texts. The Sharia is the fruit of the doctrine of political Islam.

THE WIFE'S MARITAL OBLIGATIONS

It is obligatory for a woman to let her husband have sex with her immediately when he asks her; at home; and if she can physically endure it.

If sex will harm her, she does not have to comply.

THE HUSBAND'S RIGHTS

A man has all rights to his wife's body. He is entitled to take her with him when he travels.

PERMITTING ONE'S WIFE TO LEAVE THE HOUSE

A husband may permit his wife to leave the house for religion and to see her female friends, or to go to any place in the town. A woman may not leave the city without her husband or a member of her unmarriageable kin accompanying her. All other travel is unlawful.

The husband may forbid his wife to leave the home because the Prophet said, "It is not permissible for a woman who believes in Allah and the Last Day to allow someone into her husband's house if he is opposed, or to go out if he is averse".

THE CONDITIONS THAT ENTITLE A WIFE TO SUPPORT

The husband is only obliged to support his wife when she does not refuse him sex at any time of the night or day. She is not entitled to support from her husband when she does not obey him, even if for a moment or travels without his permission.

This is the Sunna of Mohammed

---

1. Ahmad Ibn Naqib Al-Misri, *The Reliance of the Traveller, A Classic Manual of Islamic Sacred Law* (Amana Publications, 1994).

SEX

CHAPTER 4

*4:69 Those who obey Allah and His Messenger will live
with the messengers and the faithful and the martyrs
and the righteous. What wonderful company!*

- Adultery is a capital offense.
- Mohammed allowed female genital mutilation as an acceptable practice.
- A woman should not enhance her appearance.
- A woman should never be alone with any man who could be a sexual partner.

Sex outside marriage with another Muslim has serious consequences. Sex with a Kafir female does not have any strictures. Under no circumstances, including marriage, is a Muslim female to ever have sex with a Kafir.

[B1,10,504;B2,23,413;B6,60,209]

A man told Mohammed that he had kissed a woman. Through his Prophet, Allah revealed:

Koran 11:114 Observe prayer at early morning, at the close of the day, and at the approach of night, for good deeds drive away evil deeds. This is a warning for the mindful. Be patient, for Allah will not let the reward of the righteous perish.

The man asked Mohammed, "Is this instruction for me?" He said, "It is for all my followers."

When Maiz came to the Mohammed to confess adultery, the Prophet said to him, "Probably you have only kissed the lady, or winked, or looked at her?" He said, "No, O Allah's Apostle!" Mohammed said, using no euphemism, "Did you have sexual intercourse with her?" After he confessed to his crime, the Prophet ordered that he be stoned to death.

On another occasion, the Jew brought before Mohammed a man and woman who had committed adultery. He ordered both of them to be stoned to death near the place where the funeral prayers are offered beside the mosque.

SEXUAL MUTILATION

It is unfortunate that the term circumcision is applied to both the removal of the foreskin of the male and the removal of the clitoris of the woman. There is no comparison as to the effects. Circumcision does not destroy sexual pleasure for the man. However, removal of the clitoris of the female is akin to removal of the entire penis of the man.

> [B7,72,777;B7,72,778;B7,72,779]
>
> *Mohammed said, "Five practices are characteristics of the ancient prophets: circumcision, shaving the pubic hair, cutting the moustaches short, clipping the nails, and depilating the hair of the armpits."*

This hadith refers to the circumcision of female genitalia. It assumes that both the man and the woman are circumcised.

> M003,0684
>
> *An argument arose in Medina between a group of Helpers and Immigrants concerning bathing. The Helpers believed that bathing after sex was obligatory only if there is an ejaculation. The Immigrants believed that a bath is always obligatory after sex. Abu Musa said, "Let me settle the matter."*
>
> *He went to Aisha and asked and received her permission to speak. He said, "Aisha, beloved of the prophet, I want to question you about an embarrassing matter." Aisha said, "Do not be shy. Speak to me as you would your mother." Abu Musa then said, "When is a bath obligatory?" Aisha responded, "You have asked the right person. Mohammed has said that a bath is obligatory when a man is encompassed by a woman and their circumcised genitalia touch."*

Circumcision is part of the Sharia law. Here we have both the translation and an argument about the translation.

e4.3 Circumcision is obligatory for both men and women. For men it consists of removing the prepuce from the penis, and for women, removing the prepuce of the clitoris (not the clitoris itself, as some mistakenly assert). [1]

However what the Arabic actually says is:

"Circumcision is obligatory (for every male and female) by cutting off the piece of skin on the glans of the penis of the male, but

---

1   Ahmad Ibn Naqib Al-Misri, *The Reliance of the Traveller, A Classic Manual of Islamic Sacred Law* (Amana Publications, 1994).

26

circumcision of the female is by cutting out the clitoris (this is called Hufaad)."

This deceptive translation obscures the Sharia law. It is a deception is called *taqiyya*, a form of sacred deception.

At the battle of Badr, we have a reference to the custom of removing the clitoris.

1564 Hamza fought until he killed Arta who was one of those who were carrying the standard. Then Siba passed by him, and Hamza said, '*Come here, you son of a female circumciser.*' Now his mother was Umm Anmar, *a female circumciser in Mecca*. Then Hamza smote him and killed him.

The Sunna of Mohammed is that he never forbade the removal of the clitoris, a common custom of his day.

Sex is used to tell the doctrine of predestination. Islam has a dualistic theory about predestination. There is support for predestination and there is support for free will. Which is right? Both are right, that is the nature of duality.

> [B1,6,315;B4,54,430;B4,55,550;B8,77,593;B8,77,594;B9,93,546]
> *Mohammed said:*
> *Each one of you collected in your mother's womb for forty days, and then turned into a clot for forty days, and turned into a piece of flesh for a similar period of forty days.*
> *Then Allah sends an angel and orders him to write four things upon you: your livelihood, deeds, age, and whether you will be of the wretched or the blessed in the Hereafter. Then the soul was breathed into you.*
> *And by Allah, a man may do the evil deeds of the people of Hell until he is within arm's reach of Hell, but then that writing which Allah has ordered the angel to write takes precedent, and he will do the deeds of the people of Paradise and enter it. Conversely a man may do the good deeds of the people of Paradise until he is within arm's reach of Paradise, and then that writing takes precedent and he will do the deeds of the people of the Hell and enter it.*

In Islam, the only males that a female should be alone with are those she cannot marry. This limits her male relationships to family members. School, sports, career, friendships, are all determined by this hadith. Islam always assumes that if a man and a woman are alone, it is about sex.

[B4,52,250;B7,62,160]

Mohammed said, "It is not permissible for a man to be alone with a woman, and no lady should travel except with her husband or a person whom she could not possibly marry." Then a man got up and said, "O Allah's Apostle! I have enlisted in the army for jihad and my wife is proceeding for the Hajj pilgrimage to Mecca." Mohammed said, "Go, and perform the Hajj with your wife."

Although this hadith is not about the sex act, it is about sexual attractiveness.

[B7,62,133;B7,72,815;B7,72,816;B7,72,817;B7,72,818;B7,72,819;B7,72,822;B7,72,826;B7,72,829;B7,72,830;B7,72,832]

Mohammed said, "Allah has cursed the lady who artificially lengthens hair and the one who gets her hair lengthened, as well as the one who tattoos and the one who gets herself tattooed." Mohammed has also said that Allah curses women who remove hair from their faces, those who space their teeth on purpose for beauty, or any woman who changes features created by Allah.

Before sex, a Muslim should always pray for protection from Satan.

[B1,4,143;B4,54,493;B4,54,503B7,62,94;B8,75,397;B9,93,493;]

Mohammed said that when having sex with one's wife, he should say, "'In the name of Allah. O Allah! Protect us from Satan and prevent Satan from approaching our offspring that you are going to give us." If the man and his wife have a child as a result of that encounter, Satan will not harm it.

Homosexuality between women is treated more seriously than between men.

Koran 4:15 *If any of your women are guilty of lewdness [lesbianism], then bring in four of you as witnesses against them. If they admit their guilt, then shut them up in their houses until they die or until Allah makes some other way for them. If two of your men are guilty of an indecent act [homosexuality], punish both of them. If they ask for forgiveness and change their ways, then leave them alone, for Allah is forgiving and merciful!*

This is the Sunna of Mohammed

BEATING THE WIFE

CHAPTER 5

8:13 This was because they opposed Allah and His messenger. Ones who oppose Allah and His messenger will be severely punished by Allah.

- Men are superior to women.
- Men can lightly beat their wives.
- Mohammed hit one of his wives.
- Sharia law supports beating the wife.
- A wife should not be struck in the face.

If the detailed rules of marital conduct are not followed by the wife, there is sacred force. Here we have the words of the Koran:

> Koran 4:34 *Allah has made men superior to women because men spend their wealth to support them. Therefore, virtuous women are obedient, and they are to guard their unseen parts as Allah has guarded them. As for women whom you fear will rebel, admonish them first, and then send them to a separate bed, and then beat them. But if they are obedient after that, then do nothing further; surely Allah is exalted and great!*

When Mohammed gave his last sermon, he mentioned beating the wife:

> I969 He also told them men had rights over their wives and women had rights over their husbands. The wives were never to commit adultery or act in a sexual manner toward others. If they did, they were to be put in separate rooms and *beaten lightly*. If they refrained from what was forbidden, they had the right to food and clothing. Men were to lay injunctions on women lightly for they were prisoners of men and had no control over their persons.

Beating the wife is sacred because both Allah and Mohammed sanction it. The Hadith is filled with examples that establish the Sharia law about how to go about beating the wife.

In this hadith, a wife has her face bruised from being hit by her husband and goes to see Mohammed for his judgment on a marital problem.

[B3,48,807;B7,63,186;B7,63,187;B7,63,190;B7,63,238;B7,72,684;B7,72,715;B8,73,107]

Rifa divorced his wife, who then married Abdur-Rahman. The lady came to Aisha, wife of Mohammed, wearing a green veil and complained to Aisha of her husband and showed her a green spot on her skin caused by beating. It was the habit of ladies to support each other, so when Mohammed came, Aisha said, "I have not seen any woman suffering as much as Muslim women. Look! Her skin is greener than her clothes!"

When Abdur-Rahman heard that his wife had gone to Moham-med, he came with his two sons by another wife. The wife in the green veil said, "By Allah! I have done no wrong to him but he is impotent and is as useless to me as this," holding and showing the fringe of her garment, Abdur-Rahman said, "By Allah, O Allah's Apostle! She has told a lie! I am very strong and can satisfy her but she is disobedient and wants to go back to Rifa." Mohammed said to her, "If that is your intention, then know that it is unlawful for you to remarry Rifa until you have consummated your marriage with Abdur-Rahman."

Then the Prophet saw two boys with Abdur-Rahman and asked (him), "Are these your sons?" After Abdur-Rahman replied that this was so, Mohammed said to the woman, "You claim that he is impotent? But by Allah, these boys resemble him as a crow resembles a crow."

Several things should be noticed. Aisha, the favorite wife of Moham-med, calls attention to the common mistreatment of Muslim wives by their husbands. Mohammed does not condemn the beating, nor even mention it. The wife may want a divorce, but before she can get it, she must have sex with the husband she wants to leave.

In the next hadith Mohammed does not condemn the fact that Abu Jahm beats his wives.

Muslim 009, 3527;3512;3526

...She said: Muawiya and Abul-Jahm were among those who had given me the proposal of marriage. Thereupon Allah's Apostle said: Muawiya is destitute and in poor condition and Abul-Jahm beats women, you should take Osama b. Zaid as your husband.

Not only did Abul Jahm beat women, this hadith shows that using a stick to beat the wife is not disapproved by Mohammed.

M009,3512

[...] She said: When my period of iddah was over, I mentioned to him that Muawiya and Jahm had sent proposals of marriage to me, whereupon Allah's Messenger said: As for Abu Jahm, he does

not put down his staff from his shoulder, and as for Muawiya, he is a poor man having no property; marry Osama. I objected to him, but he again said: marry Osama; so I married him. Allah blessed me and I was envied by others.

In the next hadith we have part of the code for beating. A woman may be beaten, but not on the face. This contradicts the earlier hadith where Mohammed did not condemn the husband bruising his wife's face.

Abu Dawud 11, 2137
Narrated Muawiyah al-Qushayri:
Muawiyah asked: Apostle of Allah, what is the right of the wife of one of us over him? He replied: That you should give her food when you eat, clothe her when you clothe yourself, do not strike her on the face, do not revile her or separate yourself from her except in the house.

At first Mohammed said that Muslims should not beat their wives.

Abu Dawud 11, 2138; 2139
Muawiyah said: Apostle of Allah, how should we approach our wives and how should we leave them? He replied: Approach your tilth (tilth is a plowed field, a term for the vagina) when or how you will, give her (your wife) food when you take food, clothe when you clothe yourself, do not revile her face, and do not beat her.

But the men complained about wives who were not submissive enough, and had to be put in their place. When the Muslim women came to his house to complain about their beating, he condemned them, not the husbands who beat them. Physical force is always an option in Islam.

Abu Dawud 11, 2141:
Mohammed said: Do not beat Allah's handmaidens, but when Umar came to Mohammed and said: Women have become emboldened towards their husbands, Mohammed gave permission to beat them. Then many women came round the family of Mohammed complaining against their husbands.
So Mohammed said: Many women have gone round Mohammed's family complaining against their husbands. They are not the best among you.

Here we have an example of Mohammed striking his favorite wife.

Muslim 004, 2127
…When it was my turn for Allah's Messenger to spend the night with me, he turned his side, put on his mantle and took off his shoes and placed them near his feet, and spread the corner of his shawl on his bed and then lay down till he thought that I had gone to

sleep. He took hold of his mantle slowly and put on the shoes slowly, and opened the door and went out and then closed it lightly.

I covered my head, put on my veil and tightened my waist wrapper, and then went out following his steps till he reached Baqi'. He stood there and he stood for a long time. He then lifted his hands three times, and then returned and I also returned. He hastened his steps and I also hastened my steps. He ran and I too ran. He came (to the house) and I also came (to the house). I, however, preceded him and I entered (the house), and as I lay down in the bed, he (the Holy Prophet) entered the (house), and said: Why is it, O Aisha, that you are out of breath? I said: There is nothing.

He said: Tell me or Allah would inform me. I said: Messenger of Allah, may my father and mother be ransom for you, and then I told him the whole story. He said: Was it the darkness of your shadow that I saw in front of me? I said: Yes. He struck me on the chest which caused me pain, and then said: Did you think that Allah and His Apostle would deal unjustly with you?...

This hadith determines Islamic social custom and family law about wife beating.

Abu Dawud 11, 2142

Mohammed said: A man will not be asked as to why he beat his wife.

This hadith equates camels, slaves and women.

Abu Dawud 11, 2155

Mohammed said: If one of you marries a woman or buys a slave, he should say: "O Allah, I ask You for the good in her, and in the disposition You have given her; I take refuge in You from the evil in her, and in the disposition You have given her." When he buys a camel, he should take hold of the top of its hump and say the same kind of thing.

More advice about slaves and women:

[B7,62,132]

The Prophet said, "None of you should flog his wife as he flogs a slave and then have sexual intercourse with her in the last part of the day."

SHARIA LAW

The Hadith, the Sira and the Koran are all the basis of Islamic law, the Sharia. Here we see how Islamic law follows from the previous material.

DEALING WITH A REBELLIOUS WIFE[1]

m10.12 When a husband notices signs of rebelliousness in his wife whether in words as when she answers him coldly when she used to do so politely; or he asks her to come to bed and she refuses, contrary to her usual habit; or whether in acts, as when he finds her averse to him when she was previously kind and cheerful), he warns her in words without keeping from her or hitting her, for it may be that she has an excuse.

The warning could be to tell her,

"Fear Allah concerning the rights you owe to me,"

or it could be to explain that rebelliousness nullifies his obligation to support her and give her a turn amongst other wives, or it could be to inform her,

"Your obeying me is religiously obligatory".

If she commits rebelliousness, he keeps from sleeping (having sex) with her without words, and may hit her, but not in a way that injures her, meaning he may not bruise her, break bones, wound her, or cause blood to flow. It is unlawful to strike another's face. He may hit her whether she is rebellious only once or whether more than once, though a weaker opinion holds that he may not hit her unless there is repeated rebelliousness.

To clarify this paragraph, we mention the following rulings:

(1) Both man and wife are obliged to treat each other kindly and graciously.

(2) It is not lawful for a wife to leave the house except by the permission of her husband, though she may do so without permission when there is a pressing necessity. Nor may a wife permit anyone to enter her husband's home unless he agrees, even their unmarriageable kin. Nor may she be alone with a non-family-member male, under any circumstances.

(3) It is obligatory for a wife to obey her husband as is customary in allowing him full lawful sexual enjoyment of her person. It is obligatory for the husband to enable her to remain chaste and free

---

1. Ahmad Ibn Naqib Al-Misri, *The Reliance of the Traveller, A Classic Manual of Islamic Sacred Law* (Amana Publications, 1994).

of want for sex if he is able. It is not obligatory for the wife to serve her husband; if she does so, it is voluntary charity.

(4) If the wife does not fulfill one of the above mentioned obligations, she is termed "rebellious", and the husband takes the following steps to correct matters:

(a) admonition and advice, by explaining the unlawfulness of rebellion, its harmful effect on married life, and by listening to her viewpoint on the matter;

(b) if admonition is ineffectual, he keeps from her by not sleeping in bed with her, by which both learn the degree to which they need each other;

(c) if keeping from her is ineffectual, it is permissible for him to hit her if he believes that hitting her will bring her back to the right path, though if he does not think so, it is not permissible. His hitting her may not be in a way that injures her, and is his last recourse to save the family;

Examples of rebelliousness are when a wife gives a cold answer or does not submit to sex when he asks. He should not hit her but tell her, "Fear Allah concerning the rights you owe to me,"

He can explain that rebelliousness means that he does not need to support her or it could be to inform her, "Your obeying me is a religious obligation."

If she commits rebelliousness, he may hit her but not in a way that injures her, meaning he may not bruise her, break bones, wound her, or cause blood to flow. It is unlawful to strike another's face. He may hit her whether she is rebellious only once or whether more than once.

This is the Sunna of Mohammed

MOHAMMED'S WIVES

CHAPTER 6

47:33 Believers! Obey Allah and the messenger,
and do not let your effort be in vain.

- Khadija was his favorite wife.
- Aisha was the favorite wife in his harem.
- Mohammed started having sex with Aisha when she was nine.
- One of Mohammed's favorite sexual partners was a Christian slave girl.
- Two of Mohammed's wives were captive booty in jihad.

The best estimate of the number of Mohammed's wives is eleven and he had two sex slaves.

KHADIJA

Khadija married Mohammed when she was forty and he was twenty-five. She was a wealthy widow and was his only wife for twenty-five years. She died at age sixty-five, when Mohammed was fifty. They had six children, with only their daughter, Fatima, surviving Mohammed.

SAUDA

Mohammed married Sauda, a Muslim widow, two months after Khadija's death. About seven years later, she gave up her turn with Mohammed to Aisha, his favorite wife.

AISHA

Aisha was the daughter of Abu Bakr. She was engaged to Mohammed when she was six and Mohammed started having sex with her when she was nine and he was fifty-three. She was Mohammed's favorite wife and was eighteen when he died. She was two years old at the time of this dream.

[B5,58,35;B7,62,15;B7,62,57;B9,87,139;B9,87,140]
Mohammed dreamed of Aisha twice before they met. In his
dream, an angel carried a picture on a piece of silk, and the angel
said to him, "This is your wife." When he uncovered the picture,

and saw that it was Aisha's, he said, "If this is from Allah, it will be done."

Aisha's wedding night:

[B5,58,234;B5,58,236;B7,62,64;B7,62,65;B7,62,88;B7,62,90]

Mohammed became engaged to Aisha when she was six years old. She then went to Medina and stayed at the home of Bani-al-Harith, where she got ill and lost her hair. After her hair grew back by the age of nine, her mother handed her to the care of some women, who prepared her for her marriage to Mohammed. He consummated his marriage with her when she was nine years old and she remained with him for nine more years until his death.

Aisha brought her dolls into the harem. Since Mohammed hated images this was a big favor to her.

[B8,73,151]

Aisha used to play with dolls in front of Mohammed even though such acts were forbidden. She was allowed to do so before she reached the age of puberty. Her friends who played with her would hide when Mohammed entered the room, but he would call them back to resume playing with Aisha.

JUWAIRIYA

Juwairiya was a captive when Mohammed attacked her tribe. The attack was a sneak attack, a favorite of Mohammed. She was beautiful and Mohammed paid her ransom to the jihadist who owned her. He then married her. As a result, the rest of the captives of her tribe were now related to Mohammed by marriage. They were then freed as a result.

HAFSA

Hafsa was a widow and the daughter of Umar, later to be the second caliph.

ZAINAB, DAUGHTER OF KHUZAIMAH

This Zainab was the widow of Mohammed's cousin, killed at the battle of Badr. She was called the "Mother of the Poor" for her charity work. She died before Mohammed.

UMM SALAMA

Umm Salama was the widow of a jihadist killed at the battle of Uhud.

ZAINAB BINT JAHSH

Zainab was the beautiful wife of Mohammed's adopted son, Zaid. The Koran changed the Arabian incest laws so that Mohammed could marry her. She bragged to the other wives that Mohammed had chosen them, but she was chosen by Allah for Mohammed. [Her story is also in the chapter, Mohammed's Family Life.]

SAFIYA

Safiya was a beautiful Jew of Khaybar. Her husband and father were killed by Mohammed's jihad. After the battle Mohammed married her.

[B1,8,367;B2,14,68;B3,34,431;B3,34,437;B4,52,143,B5,59,512;B5,59,513;B5,59,522;B5,5 9,523;B875,374]

Anas said, 'When Allah's Apostle invaded Khaybar, we offered the Fajr prayer there yearly in the morning when it was still dark. The Prophet rode and Abu Talha rode too and I was riding behind Abu Talha. The Prophet passed through the lane of Khaybar quickly and my knee was touching the thigh of the Prophet. He uncovered his thigh and I saw the whiteness of the thigh of the Prophet.

When he entered the town, he said, 'Allahu Akbar! Khaybar is ruined. Whenever we approach near a nation to fight then evil will be the morning of those who have been warned.' He repeated this thrice. The people came out for their jobs and some of them said, 'Mohammed has come with his army.' We conquered Khaybar, took the captives, and the booty was collected.

Dihya came and said, 'O Allah's Prophet! Give me a slave girl from the captives.' He took Safiya. A man came to the Prophet and said, 'O Allah's Apostle! You gave Safiya to Dihya and she is the chief mistress of the Jews and she befits none but you.' So the Prophet said, 'Bring him along with her.' So Dihya came with her and when the Prophet saw her, he said to Dihya, 'Take any other slave girl from the captives.'

Her husband had been killed by the Muslims while she was a bride. Mohammed then proposed that she marry him. Since she was a captive she needed to be ransomed to be freed. On the other hand, Mohammed owed her a dowry. So the dowry was set equal to the ransom.

The Prophet stayed with Safiya for three days on the way from Khaybar. After three days her period was over and Um Sulaym dressed her for marriage and at night she sent her as a bride to the Prophet.

Safiya was amongst those who were ordered to use a veil.

So the Prophet was a bridegroom and he said, 'Whoever has any food should bring it.' He spread out a leather sheet for the food and some brought dates and others cooking butter. So they prepared a dish. And that was the marriage banquet of Allah's Apostle."

UMM HABIBA

Umm Habiba was the daughter of Abu Sufyan, an enemy of Mohammed. She was a widow when Mohammed married her.

MAIMUNA

Maimuna was a widow of 51 when Mohammed married her.

MARY, THE COPT

Mary was a Christian slave used for sex by Mohammed. Mary was fair skinned with wavy hair. She was the cause of a revolt of Mohammed's wives when he spent too much time with her. She had a son by him, who died at an early age.

RIHANA

Riahana was a beautiful Jewish slave used for sex by Mohammed. She became his after he executed her husband, along with eight hundred other Jewish males.

This is the Sunna of Mohammed

JEALOUSY

CHAPTER 7

*61:11 Believe in Allah and His messenger and fight valiantly
for Allah's cause [jihad] with both your wealth and your
lives. It would be better for you, if you only knew it!*

- Mary, Mohammed's sex slave, caused jealousy in the harem.
- Mohammed abandoned his wives for a month over an argument.
- The wives competed with each other over Mohammed's attention.
- All Muslims know about Mohammed's favorite wife.

A natural question arises: how did Mohammed live with all of his wives
without jealousy, tension, arguments and bad feelings? The answer is that
there were jealousy, tension, arguments and bad feelings. The family quar-
rels are reflected in all of the Trilogy.

MARY, THE COPTIC SLAVE OF PLEASURE

M425 Mohammed was given two Coptic (Egyptian Christian) slaves.
One he gave to another Muslim but he kept Mary, fair of skin with
curly hair. He did not move her into the harem, but set up an apartment in another part of Medina. Mary gave something in sex that none
of his wives could—a child and it was a male child, Ibrahim. Mohammed doted on him.

M426 The harem was jealous. This non-Arab slave had given Mohammed his best gift. One of his wives, Hafsa, was away and Mohammed
took Mary to Hafsa's apartment in the harem. Hafsa returned and there
was a scene. The harem was incensed. A slave in one of their beds was
an outrage and a scandal. The wives banded together and it was a house
of anger and coldness.

M427 Mohammed withdrew and swore he would not see his wives for
a month and lived with Mary. Omar and Abu Bakr were appalled as Mohammed, their son-in-law had abandoned their daughters for a slave. But
at last Mohammed relented and said that Gabriel had spoken well of Hafsa
and he wanted the whole affair to be over.

The Koran:

> Koran 66:1 *Why, Oh, Messenger, do you forbid yourself that which Allah has made lawful to you? Do you seek to please your wives? [Mohammed was fond of a Coptic (Egyptian Christian) slave named Mary. Hafsa found Mohammed in her room with Mary, a violation of Hafsa's domain. He told a jealous Hafsa that he would stop relations with Mary and then did not. But Hafsa was supposed to be quiet about this matter.] Allah is lenient and merciful. Allah has allowed you release from your oaths, and Allah is your master. He is knowing and wise.*
>
> Koran 66:3 *When the Messenger confided a fact to one of his wives, and when she divulged it, [Hafsa had told Aisha (Mohammed's favorite wife) about Mary and the harem became embroiled in jealousy.] Allah informed Mohammed of this, and he told her [Hafsa] part of it and withheld part. When Mohammed told her of it, she said, "Who told you this?" He said, "He who is knowing and wise told me."*
>
> Koran 66:4 *"If you both [Hafsa and Aisha] turn in repentance to Allah, your hearts are already inclined to this, but if you conspire against the Messenger, then know that Allah is his protector, and Gabriel, and every just man among the faithful, and the angels are his helpers besides. Perhaps, if he [Mohammed] divorced you all, Allah would give him better wives than you—Muslims, believers, submissive, devout, penitent, obedient, observant of fasting, widows, and virgins."*

This next hadith is one of the longest. It goes into great detail about "the secret that Hafsa told Aisha." The secret was about Mohammed's being in Hafsa's bed with the slave, Mary.

> [B3,43,648;B13,89;Bj7,72,734,B7,62,119]
>
> *Narrated Ibn Abbas:*
>
> *I had been eager to ask Umar about the two ladies from among the wives of the Prophet mentioned in the Koran.*
>
> *If you two (wives of the Prophet namely Aisha and Hafsa) turn in repentance to Allah your hearts are indeed so inclined (to oppose what the Prophet likes) (66.4),*
>
> *On our way back from Mecca Umar went to answer the call of nature and I also went aside along with him carrying a tumbler of water. When he had answered the call of nature and returned, I poured water on his hands from the tumbler and he performed ablution. I said, "O Chief of the believers! ' Who were the two ladies from among the wives of the Prophet mentioned in the Koran. He said, "I am astonished at your question, O Ibn Abbas. They were Aisha and Hafsa."*

Then Umar said. "I and neighbor of mine used to visit the Prophet in turns. He used to go one day, and I another day. When I went I would bring him the news of what had happened that day regarding the instructions and orders and when he went, he used to do the same for me.

We, the people of Mecca used to have authority over women, but when we came to live in Medina, we noticed that the Medinan women had the upper hand over their men, so our women started acting like them. Once I shouted at my wife and she shouted back at me. She said, 'Why do you take it ill that I shout at you? By Allah, the wives of the Prophet shout at him, and some of them may not speak with him for the whole day till night.' What she said scared me and I said to her, 'Whoever amongst them does so, will be a great loser.' Then I dressed myself and went to Hafsa (Umar's daughter and a wife) and asked her, 'Does any of you keep Allah's Apostle angry all the day long till night?' She replied in the affirmative. I said, 'She is a ruined losing person and will never have success! Doesn't she fear that Allah may get angry for the anger of Allah's Apostle and thus she will be ruined? Don't ask Allah's Apostle too many things, and don't talk back to him in any case, and don't desert him. Demand from me whatever you like, and don't be tempted to imitate Aisha in her behavior towards the Prophet, for she is more beautiful than you, and more beloved to Allah's Apostle.

In those days it was rumored that the Ghassan, (a tribe living in Sham) was getting prepared to invade us. My companion went to the Prophet and returned to us at night and knocked at my door violently, asking whether I was sleeping. I was scared by the hard knocking and came out to him. He said that a great thing had happened. I asked him: What is it? Have the Ghassan come? He replied that it was worse and more serious than that, and added that Allah's Apostle had divorced all his wives.

I said, 'Hafsa is a ruined loser! I expected that would happen some day.' So I dressed myself, went to the mosque and offered the Fajr prayer with the Prophet. Then the Prophet entered an upper room and stayed there alone. I went to Hafsa and found her weeping. I asked her, 'Why are you weeping? Didn't I warn you? Has Allah's Apostle divorced you all?' She replied, 'I don't know. He is there in the upper room.'

I then went out and came to the pulpit and found a group of people around it and some of them were weeping. Then I sat with them for some time, but could not endure the situation. So I went to the upper room where the Prophet was and requested to a black slave of his: "Will you get the permission for Umar to enter? The slave went in, talked to the Prophet about it and came out saying, 'I mentioned you to him but he did not reply.' So, I went and sat with the people who were sitting by the pulpit, but I could not bear the situation, so I went to the slave again and said: "Will you get permission for me? He went in and brought the same reply as before. When I was leaving, behold, the slave called me saying, "Allah's Apostle has granted you permission."

So, I entered upon the Prophet and saw him lying on a mat without bedding on it, and the mat had left its mark on the body of the Prophet, and he was leaning on a leather pillow stuffed with palm leaves. I greeted him and while still standing, I said: "Have you divorced your wives?' He raised his eyes to me and replied in the negative. And then while still standing, I said, chatting: "Will you heed what I say, 'O Allah's Apostle! We, the people of Mecca used to have the upper hand over our wives, and when we came to the people whose women had the upper hand over them."

Umar told the whole story about his wife. "On that the Prophet smiled." Umar further said, "I then said, 'I went to Hafsa and said to her: Do not be tempted to imitate Aisha for she is more beautiful than you and more beloved to the Prophet.' The Prophet smiled again. When I saw him smiling, I sat down and cast a glance at the room, and by Allah, I couldn't see anything of importance but three hides. I said to Allah's Apostle "Invoke Allah to make your followers prosperous for the Persians and the Byzantines have been made prosperous and given worldly luxuries, though they do not worship Allah?' The Prophet sat up straight and said, 'O Umar! Do you have any doubt that the Hereafter is better than this world? These people have been given rewards of their good deeds in this world only.'

I asked the Prophet, "'Please ask Allah's forgiveness for me." The Prophet did not go to his wives because of the secret which Hafsa had told to Aisha, and he said that he would not go to his wives for one month as he was angry with them. Allah admonished him for his oath that he would not approach his slave Mary, the Copt. When twenty-nine days had passed, the Prophet went to Aisha first of all. She said to him, 'You took an oath that you would not come to us for one month, and today only twenty-nine days have passed, as I have been counting them day by day.' The Prophet said, 'The month is also of twenty-nine days.' Aisha said, 'When the Divine revelation of Choice was revealed, the Prophet started with me, saying to me, 'I am telling you something, but you needn't hurry to give the reply till you can consult your *parents." Aisha knew that her parents would not advise her to part with the Prophet. The Prophet said that Allah had said:*

33:28 Messenger! Say to your wives, "If you desire a life of this world and al' its glittering adornment, then come. I will provide for you and release you with honor. If, however, you seek Allah and His Messenger and the world to come, then know that Allah has prepared a great reward for those of you who do good works.

Aisha said, 'Am I to consult my parents about this? I indeed prefer Allah, His Apostle, and the Home of the Hereafter.' After that the Prophet gave the choice to his other wives and they also gave the same reply as Aisha did."

Mary, the Copt, may have been a slave who was looked down upon by the wives, but she had the advantage of giving Mohammed a son. Soon that was lost.

M429 Ibrahim became a favorite of Mohammed. But when the child was fifteen months old, he fell sick. Mary and her slave sister attended the child during his illness. Mohammed was there at his death and wept mightily. Mohammed was to suffer the Arabic shame of having no living male children to succeed him. Mary, the Copt, disappears from the Trilogy after the death of Ibrahim.

HADITH OF JEALOUSY

Here the jealousy is between Aisha and Hafsa.

[B3,47,766;B3,48,853;B4,52,130;B7,62,138;B7,62,139]

Whenever Mohammed was preparing for a journey, he would draw lots to see which of his wives would accompany him. Also, he would fix a day and a night for each of his wives. Sauda gave her day and night to Aisha so the she might please Mohammed with this action.

During one of his journeys, the lot fell on Aisha and Hafsa, and at night Mohammed would ride beside Aisha and talk with her. One night Hafsa asked Aisha to switch camels with her, and she agreed. After Mohammed rode beside Hafsa on Aisha's camel, Aisha missed him, and when they dismounted she put her legs in the grass and said, "Oh Allah! Send a scorpion or snake to bite me for I am not to blame the Prophet."

Mohammed had to deal with jealousy among his wives.

[B7,62,152]

While Mohammed was in the house of one of his wives, one of his other wives sent a meal in a dish. The wife he was visiting at the time struck the hand of the slave, causing the dish to fall and break. Mohammed gathered the broken pieces of the dish and then started collecting on them the food which had been in the dish and said, "My wife felt jealous." Then he detained the slave until an unbroken dish was provided by the wife he was visiting. He gave the sound dish to the wife who had sent the meal and left the broken one at the house where it had been broken.

Mohammed is on his death bed. Here we have a record of a lifelong tension between Aisha and Hafsa.

[B1,11,647;B1,11,684;B9,92,406]

Narrated Aisha:

When Mohammed was in his illness said, "Tell Abu Bakr to lead the people in prayer." I said to him, "If Abu Bakr stands in your place, the people would not hear him owing to his excessive weeping. So please order Umar to lead the prayer."

Aisha added, I said to Hafsa, "Say to him: If Abu Bakr should lead the people in the prayer in your place, the people would not be able to hear him owing to his weeping; so please, order Umar to lead the prayer." Hafsa did so but Allah's Apostle said, "Keep quiet! You are verily the Companions of Joseph [a betrayer]. Tell Abu Bakr to lead the people in the prayer. " Hafsa said to Aisha, "I never got anything good from you."

Since a verse of the Koran related to Zainab, she lorded this over the other wives.

[B9,93,517]

The Verse of Al-Hijab (veiling of women) was revealed in connection with Zainab bint Jahsh. On the day of her marriage with the Prophet, he gave a wedding banquet with bread and meat; and she used to boast before other wives of the Prophet and used to say, "Allah married me to the Prophet in the Heavens."

This is the Sunna of Mohammed

MOHAMMED'S FAMILY LIFE

CHAPTER 8

48:13 We have prepared a blazing Fire for these Kafirs
who do not believe in Allah and His Messenger.

- Mohammed's favorite wife, the young Aisha, was left behind during a jihad raid and she wound up being in the company of a young Muslim man for a day. Gossip raged and accusations were whispered. The Koran finally settled the issue.
- Mohammed did not like to spend money on his family and his wives complained.
- Mohammed's devotion to his new favorite sexual partner, a Christian slave, caused an uproar among his wives.
- Mohammed fell in love with his daughter-in-law. The Koran changed Islamic marriage law so he could marry her.

Mohammed had many wives. He is the perfect model for the Muslim husband, except other Muslims are limited to four wives at a time. The Koran goes into detail about his romances.

THE LIE

When Mohammed went on his missions to attack those who resisted Islam, he took one of his wives with him. Which one got to go was determined by lots. Mohammed took Aisha with him on this trip to fight in Allah's cause in attacking the Mustaliq tribe.

I731 Now there was a problem in taking one of Mohammed's wives on an expedition and that was privacy. By now the veil had been prescribed for his wives. So the wife was not supposed to be seen or heard. To accomplish this a light cloth-covered howdah was used. Basically this was a box with a seat that could be mounted on a camel's saddle. On the way back on the expedition Aisha had gone out in the morning to relieve herself. When she got back she discovered that she had lost a necklace and went back to find it. The tent had been struck and the men in charge loaded the howdah on the camel and off they went without Aisha.

1732 When Aisha got back the entire group had moved on. She returned on a camel lead by a young Muslim who had lagged behind the main body and brought her back to Medina.

1732 Tongues began to wag, imaginations worked overtime and gossip spread. Aisha fell ill and was bedridden for three weeks.

1734-5 Tempers flared and men offered to kill the gossips. Something had to be done. Mohammed asked for advice from Ali, who said, "Women are plentiful and you can easily exchange one for the other. Ask the slave girl, she will tell the truth." So Mohammed called in the slave girl and stood by while Ali severely beat her. Ali said, "Tell the apostle the truth." The slave said that she knew of nothing bad about Aisha except she could be lazy about house work.

In the end the innocence or guilt of Aisha was determined by revelation in the Koran which to this day is the Sharia (Islamic law) about adultery.

> Koran 24:1 *A sura [chapter] which We have sent down and ordained, and in which We give you clear signs so that you will take warning. The man and woman who commit adultery should each be beaten with a hundred lashes, and do not let your pity for them prevent you from obeying Allah. If you believe in Allah and the Last Day, then allow some of the believers to witness their punishment. An adulterer can only marry an adulteress or a Kafir, and a adulteress cannot marry anyone other than an adulterer or a Kafir. Such marriages are forbidden for believers.*
>
> Koran 24:4 *Those who make accusations against honorable women and are unable to produce four witnesses should be given eighty lashes. Thereafter, do not accept their testimony, for they are terrible sinners, except those who repent afterwards and live righteously. Allah is truly forgiving and merciful.*
>
> Koran 24:6 *If a husband accuses his wife of adultery but he has no witnesses other than himself, his evidence can be accepted if he swears by Allah four times that he is telling the truth and then calls down Allah's curse upon him if he is lying. If, however, the wife swears by Allah four times that she is innocent and calls Allah's curse down upon herself if she is lying, then she should not be punished.*
>
> Koran 24:10 *If it were not for Allah's grace and mercy towards you and that Allah is wise, this would not have been revealed to you.*
>
> Koran 24:11 *Truly there is a group among you who spread that lie, but do not think of it as a bad thing for you for it has proved to be advantageous for you. Every one of them will receive the punishment they have earned. Those who spread the gossip will receive a torturous punishment.*
>
> Koran24:12 *Why did the believing men and women, when they heard this, not think better of their own people and say, "This is an obvious lie"? Why*

did they not bring four witnesses? And because they could not find any witnesses, they are surely liars in Allah's sight.

Koran 24:14 *If it were not for Allah's goodness towards you and His mercy in this world and the world to come, you would have been severely punished for the lie you spread. You [the Muslims] gossiped about things you knew nothing about. You may have thought it to be only a light matter, but it was a most serious one in Allah's sight. And why, when you heard it, did you not say, "It is not right for us to talk about this. Oh, Allah! This is a serious sin." Allah warns you never to repeat this if you are true believers. Allah makes His signs clear to you, for Allah is all-knowing, wise. Those who take pleasure in spreading foul rumors about the faithful will be severely punished in this world and the world to come. And Allah knows, while you do not.*

Koran 24:20 *If it were not for Allah's grace and mercy towards you, you would have been punished long ago, but know that Allah is kind and merciful.*

Koran 24:21 *Believers, do not follow in Satan's footsteps for those who do so will be commanded to commit shameful and evil acts. If it were not for Allah's grace, not one of you would be pure. And Allah purifies those He pleases, and Allah is all-hearing.*

Koran 24:22 *And do not allow those among you who are wealthy and have many possessions to swear that they will not give to their family, the poor, and those who have fled their homes for Allah's cause [jihad]. Instead, let them be forgiving and indulgent. Do you not want Allah to show you forgiveness? Allah is forgiving and merciful.*

Koran 24:23 *Truly, those who carelessly slander believing women will be cursed in this world and the world to come. Their own tongues, hands, and feet will one day testify against them concerning their own actions. On that day Allah will give them what they have earned, and they will know that Allah is the clear truth.*

Since there were not four witnesses, then there was no adultery and the gossips got eighty lashes.

1736 But the scandal did not end here. One of those who got flogged for gossip was a poet and propagandist for the Muslim cause. The young warrior who led Aisha's camel was in a poem written by the poet and was offended. So he took his sword and cut the poet badly. The poet and his friends managed to bind the young warrior and take him to Mohammed. Mohammed wanted this to all go away. He gave the wounded poet a nice home and a Christian slave girl of pleasure as compensation for the sword blow.

MARRIAGE TO HIS DAUGHTER-IN-LAW

M290 Mohammed had an adopted son, Zaid, and went by his house. Zaid was not there and Mohammed went on in the house. He wound up seeing his daughter-in-law, Zeinab, in a thin dress, and her charms were evident. Mohammed was smitten and said, "Gracious Lord! Good Heavens! How thou dost turn the hearts of men!"

M290 Well, Zeinab, had turned the head of the future king of Arabia and she told her husband what Mohammed said. The step-son went to Mohammed and said that he would divorce Zeinab so he could have her. Mohammed said no. But Zaid went ahead and divorced her anyway. In Arabia a union between a man and his daughter-in-law was incest and forbidden. But while Mohammed was with Aisha, he had a revelation and said, "Who will go and congratulate Zeinab and tell her that Allah has blessed our marriage?" The maid went right off to tell her of the good news. So Mohammed added another wife.

> Koran 33:4 *Allah has not given any man two hearts for one body, nor has He made your wives whom you divorce to be like your mothers, nor has He made your adopted sons like your real sons. [Previous to this verse, an Arab's adopted children were treated as blood children. This verse relates to verse 37 of this sura.] These are only words you speak with your mouths, but Allah speaks the truth and guides to the right path. Name your adopted sons after their real fathers; this is more just in Allah's sight. But if you do not know their fathers' names, call them your brothers in the faith and your friends. There will be no blame on you if you sin unintentionally, but that which you intend in your heart will be held against you. Allah is forgiving and merciful.*
>
> Koran 33:36 *And it is not the place of a believer, either man or woman, to have a choice in his or her affairs when Allah and His Messenger have decided on a matter. Those who disobey Allah and His Messenger are clearly on the wrong path. And remember when you said to your adopted son [Zaid], the one who had received Allah's favor [converted to Islam], "Keep your wife to yourself and fear Allah," and you hid in your heart what Allah was to reveal, and you feared men [what people would say if he married his daughter-in-law], when it would have been right that you should fear Allah. And when Zaid divorced his wife, We gave her to you as your wife, so it would not be a sin for believers to marry the wives of their adopted sons, after they have divorced them. And Allah's will must be carried out.*
>
> Koran 33:38 *The Messenger will not be blamed for anything that Allah has given him permission to do. This was Allah's way with the messengers who came before you, and Allah's commands are absolute. The messengers fulfilled Allah's mission and feared Him, and feared no one but Allah. Allah*

takes sufficient account. Mohammed is not the father of any man among you. He is Allah's Messenger and the last of the messengers. Allah knows all things.

Since Zaid was adopted, he was not really a son, so there was no incest.

[B9,93,516]

Zaid, Mohammed's step-son, came to Mohammed complaining about his wife. The Prophet kept on saying to him, "Be afraid of Allah and keep your wife."

Aisha said, "If Allah's Apostle were to conceal anything of the Koran he would have concealed this verse [33:36, above]."

Zainab used to boast before the wives of the Prophet and used to say, "You were given in marriage by your families, while I was married to the Prophet by Allah from over seven Heavens."

FATIMA

Mohammed had several children, but none of them survived him except for Fatima, the daughter of his first wife, Khadija.

[B4,53,325;B5,57,60;B5,59,546;B8,80,718]

After Mohammed died, his daughter Fatima asked Abu Bakr to give her a share of Mohammed's estate. Abu Bakr explained that Mohammed had ordered that his property be donated to charity, so Fatima became angry and stopped speaking to him. She kept this attitude until she died six months later.

This is the Sunna of Mohammed

SEXUAL SLAVERY

CHAPTER 9

24:54 Say: Obey Allah and the Messenger.

- Having sex with your female slaves is a moral good.
- A married slave can be used for sex.
- The captives of jihad can be used for sex.
- Mohammed always got the pick of the captives to be used for sex.

For a Muslim to have sex with his slaves is in the same moral category as being humble, telling the truth or giving to charity. There is no blame and it is a moral good since it is allowed by the Koran. Allah only allows good. Sex with your slaves is only good for the male Muslim. Of course, for the female Muslim, it is a great sin.

There is a great advantage of having sex with slaves. None of the restrictions of sex apply to the slave, except for sex during the slave's menstrual period. Other than that, anything goes.

> Koran 23:1 *The successful ones will be the believers who are humble in their prayers who avoid vain conversation, who contribute to the needy, and who abstain from sex, except with their wives or slaves, in which case they are free from blame, but those who exceed these limits are sinners. Those who honor their promises and contracts and who pay strict attention to their prayers will inherit Paradise. They will dwell there forever.*

If the slave is married, then it is still morally good for a Muslim to have sex with her.

> Koran 4:24 *Also forbidden to you are married women unless they are your slaves. This is the command of Allah. Other than those mentioned, all other women are lawful to you to court with your wealth and with honorable intentions, not with lust. And give those you have slept with a dowry, as it is your duty. But after you have fulfilled your duty, it is not an offense to make additional agreements among you. Truly Allah is knowing and wise!*

The above verse was given at the time of the jihad at Khaybar. Mohammed attacked the Jews of Khaybar and conquered them. The Jews that survived were doomed to become *dhimmis*. A dhimmi is not a Muslim, but one who has agreed to do all things as Islam wishes. In this case the surviving Jews were to work the land and give half of the proceeds to the jihadists. In addition, some women were taken as sex slaves. Mohammed, after taking the most beautiful Jew for his own pleasure, laid out the rules for sex with the captives.

- The marriage of the captive woman is annulled, as per the above Koran verse.
- Don't rape a pregnant slave. Wait until she has delivered.
- Don' have sex with a woman who is having her period.

1758 Dihya had asked Mohammed for Safiya, and when he chose her for himself Mohammed gave Safiya's two cousins to Dihya in exchange. *The women of Khaybar were distributed among the Muslims.*

1759 A man said, 'Let me tell you what I heard the apostle say on the day of Khaybar. He got up among us and said: "It is not lawful for a Muslim *to mingle his seed with another man's [meaning to have sex with a pregnant woman among the captives], nor is it lawful for him to take her until he has made sure that she is in a state of cleanness [not having her period].*

Here we see that at first the jihadists were reluctant to have sex with the captive women because of their husbands being nearby. But the Koran established that it was not immoral for them to rape Kafir women because they had husbands.

> M008, 3432
>
> *Mohammed sent an army to Autas and encountered the enemy and fought with them. Having overcome them and taken them captives, the Companions seemed to refrain from having intercourse with captive women because of their husbands being polytheists. Then Allah, Most High, sent down regarding that: "And women already married, except those whom your right hands possess (iv. 24)" (i. e. they were lawful for them when their menstral period came to an end).*

JIHAD AND SEXUAL SLAVERY

The use of women for sex after jihad is a constant in the Hadith and the Sira. Here the men are asking about *coitus interruptus* to avoid pregnancy in the sex slaves. If they were pregnant, they had no value on the market as a sex slave. A Muslim is not supposed to have sex with a woman who is carrying another man's child, as per the Koran.

51

[B3,34,432;B7,62,137;B8,77,600]

Once some of Mohammed's soldiers asked if it was acceptable to use coitus interruptus to avoid impregnating the female captives they had received as their share of the booty.

Mohammed asked, "Do you really do that?" He repeated the question three times, then said: "It is better for you not to do it, for there is no soul which Allah has ordained to come into existence but will be created."

Notice that Jadd assumes that the Muslims will be raping after they win the battle. That was the normal and expected behavior.

1894 One day when Mohammed was making his arrangements for the upcoming battle and said to Jadd: 'Would you like to fight the B. Asfar, Jadd?' He replied, 'Will you allow me to stay behind and not tempt me, for everyone knows that I am strongly addicted to women and I am afraid that if I see the Byzantine women I shall not be able to control myself.'

If it were not for the cruelty of jihad, this next story has some humor. The female captive might bring a high ransom due to her high status. Mohammed said that he was going to return all of the captives at a price of six camels. Vyayna felt that she was worth more than that. His companions point out that she has no value for sex, she is not a virgin nor a plump matron.

1878 Vyayna took an old woman of Hawazin as a captive and said as he took her, 'I see that she is a person of standing in the tribe and her ransom may well be high.' When Mohammed returned the captives at a price of six camels each, Vyayna refused to give her back. Zuhayr told him to let her go, for her mouth was cold and her breasts flat; she could not conceive and her husband would not care and her milk was not rich. So he let her go for the six camels when Zuhayr said this. They allege that when Vyayna met al-Aqra later he complained to him about the matter and he said: By God, you didn't take her as a virgin in her prime nor even a plump middle-aged matron!'

Jihad can be ugly:

1980 When Zayd had raided the Fazara tribe, he and others were injured. Zayd swore he would never have sex until he had avenged his injuries. When he was well, Mohammed sent him against the Fazara. He was successful and captured some of the women. One of them was an old woman, Umm Qirfa, who husband he had killed. Zayd tied a rope to each leg of Umm Qirfa and tied each rope to a camel and pulled her apart. Her daughter was taken captive and passed around to three different men to use as they would for their pleasure.

Here is another situation in jihad where Mohammed got a new sexual partner.

> [B3,46,717]
> *Ibn Aun wrote a letter to Nafi. Nafi wrote in reply that the Prophet had suddenly attacked Bani Mustaliq tribe without warning while they were heedless and their cattle were being watered at the places of water. Their fighting men were killed and their women and children were taken as captives; the Prophet got Juwairiya on that day.*

Mohammed's love for one of his slaves, Mary, caused an uproar in his harem. Mohammed was fond of a Coptic (Egyptian Christian) slave named Mary. Hafsa found Mohammed in her room with Mary, a violation of Hafsa's domain. He told a jealous Hafsa that he would stop relations with Mary and then did not. But Hafsa was supposed to be quiet about this matter. But the Koran points out to his wives and Muslims that he can have sex with his slaves as he wishes. Therefore, when he told Hafsa he would quit, he was not bound by that oath.

> Koran 66:1 *Why, Oh, Messenger, do you forbid yourself that which Allah has made lawful to you? Do you seek to please your wives? Allah is lenient and merciful. Allah has allowed you release from your oaths, and Allah is your master. He is knowing and wise.*

And last, but not least, after life is over, Muslims will still be having sex with slaves.

> Hadith 101, Ibn Arabi, *Mishkat*
> *[...]*
> *Allah says to the Muslims in Paradise: Go to your slave-girls and concubines in the garden of Paradise.*
> *[...]*

This is the Sunna of Mohammed

COMMENTS

CHAPTER 10

SUBMISSION

The doctrine concerning women is based upon the principle of submission. Islam is a civilization of submission. The subjugation of women shows Islam's internal politics of dualism and it's doctrine of slavery shows its external politics of dualism.

Submission is always about the master/slave relationship. Allah is the master of the Muslim slaves. The Muslim male is the master of the Muslim female. The Islamic Trilogy defines the roles of a man and a woman and how they relate to each other and the world.

The submission of the woman can be measured easily. Each hadith and verse dictates the status and place of a woman in the world and in relation to a man. We can go through and categorize each verse and hadith into one of four categories for the woman, superior, equal, neutral and inferior. Superior means that the woman is held in high regard. Equal is equal power with the man. Neutral is a mention of women that does not imply any power relationship. Inferior means that the woman is controlled by the man, under his power and beneath him. The data is shown in the chart:

FIGURE 10.1: STATUS OF WOMEN IN THE HADITH (331 HADITHS)

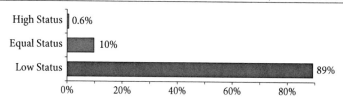

FIGURE 10.2: STATUS OF WOMEN IN THE KORAN (12,066 WORDS)

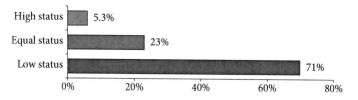

54

The only way that a Muslim woman is superior to a man is by being a mother.

The equality issue is interesting. Woman are equal to men only in that both sexes will be judged equally on Judgment Day. But there is a catch. All will be judged upon the basis of how well they have followed the laws and rules of Islam. Since most of these rules include submitting to men, the woman's equality is based on how well she submitted to men.

The results are clear. An Islamic woman must submit to a Muslim man in all things—family, business, religion, work, war, sex, law, her behavior during her menstrual cycle, travel, relationships, and marriage. Submission is Islam. Submission is Sunna. Submission is the way of Allah.

For someone from the civilization of unitary ethics based on the Golden Rule, these results seem misogynistic or anti-female. Unitary ethics strives for equality of the sexes, not submission. In Islam submission is not negative, but a summation of the right order of the Islamic world. Allah made the woman subordinate to the man in most things.

But there is also a bright light for the Islamic woman. Islam uses a dualistic logic, so that one thing does not cancel out the other, as it would if you took an average of the results. Each category stands on its own and can be used when needed, thus a summary statement cannot be made about a dualistic system. For clarity only statistics can be used. It is not true that a woman is inferior to a man in Islam. This denies the truth of the fact that she is superior 4% of the time. But it can be said that she is inferior to the male 91% of the time.

So a Muslim woman proudly points to the verses that make her an equal and is elated that the mother is superior to all men.

Dualism means that both sides of the paradox are correct. Things that are contradictory are both true.

The Muslim woman may submit to the man in all things, but she is totally equal to the Muslim man. This is dualistic Islamic logic. Also, the Muslim woman has full knowledge that she is superior to the Kafir male. Kafir males, like Kafir females, must one day submit to the Islamic woman. So the women of Islam are happy in their position in life. In a civilization of submission, submission is good.

It is simply a question of who is submitting to whom. The Muslim male has submitted to rules of all the Hadith and is a slave of Allah. Islam is one vast slave plantation with a precise hierarchy. Allah is at the top, with the Kafir slaves at the bottom, and the Muslim slaves are in the middle.

The submission of women produces peace and tranquility. A common Arabic term for a woman is *fitna*, sedition, disorder or chaos. If the woman were equal in all things, it would produce fitna. Equality is not possible in a civilization of duality and submission. Attempts at equality produce chaos. The peace of Islam comes through submission. When the woman submits, there is peace and order in society.

AL GHAZALI

One of Islam's greatest scholars was Al Ghazali, a Sufi mystic called the "proof of Islam". He summarized the state of women[1].

As for the distinctive characteristics with which God on High has punished women, the matter is as follows:

When Eve disobeyed Almighty God and ate fruit which He had forbidden to her from the tree in Paradise, the Lord, be He praised, punished women with eighteen things:
(i) menstruation;
(ii) childbirth;
(iii) separation from mother and father and marriage to a stranger;
(iv) pregnancy through him;
(v) having no control over her own person;
(vi) having a lesser share in inheritance;
(vii) her liability for being divorced and her inability to divorce;
(viii) it is lawful for men to have four wives, but for a woman to have only one husband;
(ix) the fact that she must stay secluded in the house;
(x) the fact that she must keep her head covered inside the house;
(xi) (the fact that) two women's testimonies have to be set against the testimony of one man;
(xii) the fact that she must not go out of the house unless accompanied by a near relative;
(xiii) the fact that men take part in Friday and Feast Day prayers and funerals while women do not;
(xiv) disqualification for rulership and judgeship;
(xv) the fact that merit has one thousand components, only one of which is attributable to women, while nine hundred and ninety nine are attributable to men;
(xvi) the fact that if women are profligate, they will be given only half as much torment as the rest of the Muslim community at the Resurrection Day;

1. Al-Ghazali, *Counsel for Kings*, translated F. R. C. Bagley (Oxford University Press, 1964) 164-65.

(xvii) the fact that if their husbands die, they must observe a waiting period of four months and ten days before remarrying;

(xviii) the fact that if their husbands divorce them, they must observe a waiting period of three months or three menstruation periods before remarrying.

MOLESTATION OF THE MIND

The Kafirs accept violence and threats from Islam without protest. Nowhere is this clearer than in Kafirs' acceptance of the Islamic doctrine and practice of oppressing women. There is almost no profile of society that will allow talk about Islam and women. Male/female, Christian/Jew/Hindu/atheist, white/black, media/schools/politics, no segment talks about the horror, since that would be Islamophobic. A vast immoral indifference is induced by Kafirs' fear of Islam.

This acceptance of violence is the sign of a profoundly molested psyche. The Kafir world, in particular its intellectuals and feminists, are classic manifestations of the abused wife and the abused child. Western feminists are the abused children of Islam. While jihadists in Africa rape women and cut out the clitoris of the new slave women, our feminists say little. There is no act so vile or degrading of women that Western feminists cannot ignore. Western feminists' ignorance is only exceeded by their moral bankruptcy.

They deliberately ignore the Islamic doctrine of women and do not teach it in any courses. Feminist professors rarely study wife beating in the Muslim immigrant community. The history of using women as sex slaves is not taught in either public, private or church schools. The horrors of dhimmitude, slavery and civilizational annihilation are not taught as well.

As the number of Muslims immigrate into Europe, the rape of European women goes up. It is considered racist to face this problem by acknowledging it.

Our feminist, gender intellectuals are the abused children of Islam. They are quiet, don't complain and placate the abuser.

THE CIVILIZATION OF ISLAM

The biggest single mistake that a Kafir makes is to consider Islam as a religion. Nothing about the religion of Islam affects the Kafir, except that the Kafir does not get to go to Islamic Paradise. Islam is much more than a religion. Islam is an entire civilization composed of politics, law, ethics, philosophy, logic, art, culture and religion.

It is the politics of Islam that impacts the Kafir, not the religion. The September 11 attack on the World Trade Towers was a political act of jihad. The attack had a religious motivation, but the act itself was a political act. As a matter of fact, the Islamic religion explicitly forbids a Muslim ever taking part in any religious act with the Kafir. Politics is what Islam does to the Kafirs, how it views and treats them.

A WAR OF CIVILIZATIONS

Islam is a civilization of dualism and submission. Ours is a civilization with a unitary ethical ideal. We fall short, but our ideal can be used to judge and guide us. The Golden Rule leads us to equality and freedom. Equality and freedom have no basis in duality and submission. You can't submit and be free. There is no equality in submission.

The vision that humanity is one spirit has no compromise with the vision that all the world must submit to Islam. One or the other must triumph.

For 1400 years Islam has triumphed over the Kafir, the Christian Kafir, the Jewish Kafir, the Hindu Kafir, the Buddhist Kafir, the atheist Kafir and the African Kafir.

Today our culture stumbles in the darkness of dhimmitude. But the light of knowledge of the doctrine and history of political Islam can dispel this darkness of dhimmitude.

Once we understand the true nature of the civilization of Islam, we can unite and overcome dualism and triumph over submission.

CPSIA information can be obtained
at www.ICGtesting.com
Printed in the USA
FSOW02n0158211216
28754FS

9 780979 579493